"From the start, Randy has been instrumental in helping me bring the UAB football program back. This coach's devotional book is a great testimony for everyone involved."

Bill Clark
Head Football Coach UAB

"Randy cares about the character and the future of the players he coaches and gets great pleasure out of elevating kids and families to the next level. This book, "Deep in the Heart" can help a lot of people."

Tim Alexander
Director of Character Education
UAB Football

"Randy ultimately is most concerned with the eternal fate of the players he coaches. Deep in the Heart speaks directly to that most important issue."

Tavon Arrington
Director of UAB Fellowship of Christian Athletes

"Randy Pippin's deep passion for personal development of the people he coaches makes for a compelling story. Deep in the Heart is a great read for one who wants to be entertained and enlightened with some anecdotal doses of how the gospel can be practically applied to real life and the chaotic world of coaching."

Grant Teaff
Executive Director Emeritus
American Football Coaches Association

"Randy has helped a lot of kids and families throughout Texas and Oklahoma. He truly coaches to change lives." The book "Deep in the Heart" is a Game Changer!

DW Rutledge-Retired THSCA Legend
Co-Author "Coaching to Change Lives"

"In 42 years of coaching I have not seen a better Daily Devotion book for coaches and athletes than "Deep in the Heart" by Randy Pippin who is a true example of a Christian coach and family man".

Dennis Parker THSCA Legendary Coach
and Co Author "Coaching to Change Lives"

"This is a culture-changing book and movie someday."

John Norman
CCO-Havas

"There are great, inspiring books about sports stars and other books about the Star of Eternity, Jesus Christ. This book combines both themes into an exciting and inspirational story that is Life-Changing."

Dr Larry Keefauver
Best Selling Author/International Teacher

"Deep in the Heart is an amazing and inspirational book for those who love sports and God. In this incredible story, author and coach Randy Pippin shares in great detail how the UAB football program was miraculously brought back to life after being completely shut down. Coach Pippin did more than just tell the story, he lived it and actually helped to bring the football program back to UAB. Everyone is going to find something in this story that will help them to see the possibilities even when they are not visible. Great job Coach Pippin, it was our pleasure to publish and promote this story."

Donald Newman,
Executive Director of Publishing,
Xulon Press Publishing Company

Xulon Press
2301 Lucien Way #415
Maitland, FL 32751
407.339.4217
www.xulonpress.com

Printed in the United States of America.

ISBN-13: 978-1-6305-0104-4

Deep in the Heart

Deep in my heart, *Faith*, *Family*, and *Football* have always sequentially been the most important priorities in my life. As a freshmen at Cisco Junior College, God planted a seed in my mind and heart to someday make a movie or write a book enitled "Deep in the Heart" largely in part about the "why" of football being so important to Texas boys like myself. I eventually would learn that it wasn't just Texas boys, but the South where the passion for football ran so deep.

Fast forward thirty plus years to the summer of 2015. I went to work for a newly resurrected UAB football program after I had run a guantlet through small college coaching jobs throughout the South. It started to dawn on me that I could create the framework of the book "Deep in the Heart" by logging the UAB Football "real life" events in chapter format and then documenting the chapters along the way. I knew that God was at work and a miracle was in the making, so I began to organize my thoughts on paper and blend them with the "Deep in the Heart" unfolding script.

I then went back and filled in the blanks so to speak. All along I had been living out the stories and the emotions attached to the events and the people involved through my various coaching, recruiting, and retention duties at UAB.

If you are viewing this book electronically and have an internet connection on your device, I would encourage you to click on or paste the URLs into your browser or if you are reading a hard copy simply put your phone camera over the QR Codes to pop up various short videos and articles which powerfully speak to the corresponding themes of their respective chapters.

If you are not familiar with activating QR Codes in order to activate links then follow these simple steps:

1.   OPEN phone camera.
2.   POINT viewfinder at the QR Code and adjust distance until there is a frame around code and a link pops up on your screen.
3.   TAP the link and it will take you to a video or print content.
     •   Some sites have commercials so be patient or skip them

The purpose for this "hot link feature" is to:

1.   *Establish a mood and manner to better understand the spirit of what we want the readers to "feel" in this book.*
2.   *Document events so the reader understands that we are dealing in truth and can be inspired by the fact that there is real hope in real life.*

Dynamic 3-D Living Book
Daily Documented Devotions

A daily devotional program for your personal development inspired by southern football history and the UAB football program's death, burial, resurrection, return and future.

You Can...

- Experience it all digitally with internet connection.
- Read and QR Scan Video Content with your phone and internet connection.
- Just read it.

Customized Chapter Devotions based on how long you have to spend on a chapter on any given day:

1. 5 Minutes Title, Intro Video and Picture for visual aid
2. 10 Minutes = #1 + Scripture for meditation
3. 20 Minutes = #2 + Narrative for understanding
4. 30 Minutes = #3 + Documentary for facts
5. 40 Minutes = #4 + Worship Song for inspiration
6. 50 Minutes = #5 + Reflection Questions/Prayer Guide/ Coaching Point for personalizing
7. 1 Hour+ = #6 + Video Message for enlightening
8. 1.5 Hour+ = #7 + Proverbs Chapter for wise application

RANDY PIPPIN

DAILY DOCUMENTED DEVOTIONS
FOR YOUR PERSONAL GROWTH

*Inspired by Southern Football History, Death,
Burial, Resurrection, Return, and Future*

Acknowledgments and Dedication

This book and everything associated with it is the result of a lot of people's literary and creative work. We want to give credit to everyone deserving of credit, but inevitably even with the long list to follow there will be someone inadvertently left out because these stories are so deeply rooted. So, if you are one due credit in this book but are not mentioned, please know that it is not intentional and make us aware of your content used in this book by sending me an email at randy@pipsconsulting.com so we can document your contribution and put it in the next reprint. Special thanks to the following content contributors:

Kevin Scarbinsky who not only wrote a lot but really inspired me to finish this project along with our information specialist William Johnston II.

Dr. Larry Keefauver, Don Newman, Dr. Lynn Artz and Norman Jetmundsen each gave me high levels of encouragement and finishing power.

The Greater Birmingham Area Community including UAB.

UAB Football comprised of the families of Coaches, Players, Support Staff, Alumni, Fans, and Friends of the program.

Every author, singer, songwriter, photographer, or other creative professional that is linked up in this book making it great.

> *"May these words of my mouth and this meditation of my heart be pleasing in your sight, LORD, my Rock and my Redeemer."* (Psalm 19:14)

I especially dedicate this book to the women in my life and the women in the lives of every person that the theme of this book has ever or will ever touch.

I personally owe the most to my precious wife, Sally, who has truly endured **chaos** to the point of sainthood. God bless her as she has blessed me, our children, grandchildren, and so many people along the way. There are many crowns in Heaven awaiting her and a few here on earth before it is all said and done.

I love and appreciate Sally along with our daughters Natalie, Holly, and Libby, and our granddaughter Gracie who each manifest themselves as the ultimate blessings of our love and marriage.

I also need to say, "Thank You, Lord" for my mother, Mary Lee Pippin, who took me from the jaws of dysfunctional chaos as a child and positioned me to be who I am. May she and my mother-in-law, Betty Horton, rest in peace as they cheer us on in the heavenly realms.

God has blessed us all with special women who have demonstrated extraordinary selflessness and who each of us love and are forever indebted too deep in the heart.

I challenge you to allow the periodic angelic voices that you will hear as you experience this book to remind and fill your soul with the blessing that women are to us all.

> *She is clothed with strength and dignity; she can laugh*
> *at the days to come.*
> *She speaks with wisdom, and faithful instruction is on*
> *her tongue.*
> *She watches over the affairs of her household and does*
> *not eat the bread of idleness.*
> *Her children arise and call her blessed; her husband*
> *also, and he praises her:*
> *Many women do noble things, but you surpass them all.*
> *Charm is deceptive, and beauty is fleeting; but a*
> *woman who fears the* LORD *is to be praised.*
> *Honor her for all that her hands have done, and*
> *let her works bring her praise at the city gate.*
> (Proverbs 31:25-31)

Table of Contents

Prologue: Deep in the Heart of a Southern Man xix

1. Southern Culture and Stars 1
2. The University of the South Legendary Train Ride. 8
3. John Heisman-Auburn-Clemson-Georgia Tech
    History 14
4. Birmingham and Legion Field: The Epicenter for This
    Way of Life. 21
5. Roots of UAB Athletics. 27
6. Bear Bryant and Eddie Robinson Types 32
7. The Iron Bowl and Legion Field Legendary 39
8. Roots of UAB Football 45
9. A Little Bit of Blazer History 53
10. Bill Clark 58
11. One Play vs. Marshall 64
12. Southern Miss Finale 71
13. The Shutdown. 76
14. Scattered Abroad. 81
15. How'd This Happen? 88
16. #The Return 95
17. The Staff, The Originals, and Hope for the Future 102
18. Resurrecting Opportunities 108
19. Greg Bryant Murdered. 114

20. Rising from the Ashes in Preparation 119

21. Recruiting the Dudes 124

22. Retaining the Dogs 130

23. New House 138

24. Locked, Loaded and Eligible...Picked Last 145

25. House Party. 153

26. The City Rejoices...The Return...Kickoff. 159

27. Games 1-6 and Homecoming for the Children 164

28. Games 7-12 Finishing What We Brought Back. 170

29. The Bahamas Bowl and Looking Beyond. 175

30. 2018-19 Regular Seasons...Wow 181

31. 2018-19 Championship Seasons...Wow 188

32. Resurrection Story to be Continued...

    Worldwide...You In?. 194

33. Inside These Lines...Can We Resolve Social Unrest? 199

Epilogue: Who Will Go? 203

This inspiring saga...

"Deep in the Heart" Starring UAB Football is an unprecedented, inspiring true story.

"Deep in the Heart" Starring UAB Football is a thirty-three-chapter book formulating thirty-three Bible-based devotional stories partially inspired by the UAB football team's death, burial, resurrection, return and future.

"Deep in the Heart" Starring UAB Football is most likely going to be the most unique book that you have ever experienced.

"Deep in the Heart" Starring UAB Football has been formatted with multifaceted ways to engage you.

Each chapter is a divinely inspired title, mood setting video link, picture, applicable scripture, narrative, documented story, worship song, anecdotal questions sequence, an open-ended prayer and a coaching point. Each chapter ends with a corresponding chapter from Proverbs. This format is simply all designed for the reader's own personal spiritual growth.

As a bonus feature, there are links to five southern born and bred pastors' video messages throughout the book. Chris Hodges, Senior Pastor for Highland Church of Alabama opens the book in the "Prologue" segment presenting a "Running with the Giants" message for you to refer back to as you progress through this living book and the saints in heaven cheer you on.

Houston, Texas, Pastor Joel Osteen's message links will close ten selected chapters. Links to messages from Edmond, Oklahoma

Life Church, Senior Pastor Craig Groeschel, The Potter's House, Senior Pastor TD Jakes headquartered in Dallas, Texas, and Mathews North Carolina Elevation Church, Pastor Steven Furtick will be available to access in other selected chapters. These incredible messages will enhance and enlighten the chapter themes as well as encourage and inspire you. Each of the first thirty-one chapters conclude with the numerical corresponding book of Proverbs to impart a daily dose of wisdom.

The book has initially been released in Ebook form so readers can engage in video content while reading. Thereafter, the book's release in hardcover version has a QR Code system built in so the reader can concurrently engage in the video content with their cellular phone.

Read and experience this uniquely formatted powerful ongoing story of the heart.

We believe that if you truly experience what God does in this book, you will never be the same. Our prayer is that "Deep in the Heart Starring UAB Football" will move your soul in a positive manner prompting you to positively move towards reaching the fullness of your own God-given Star Power as never before.

Even if daily is not possible, set aside a regular time and place to read and change your life in Jesus' name.

Prologue

Deep in the Heart of a Southern Man

Now faith is confidence in what we hope for and assurance about what we do not see. This is what the ancients were commended for. By faith we understand that the universe was formed at God's command, so that what is seen was not made out of what was visible. (Hebrews 11:1-3)

"Power Within" Video

One of my favorite dedications on the planet is at Cottage Hill Christian Academy School K-8 in Mobile, Alabama. There is a beautiful and bold oak tree next to the playground there at Cottage Hill that has a plaque beside it that simply says, "ONLY GOD CAN MAKE A TREE." 6th grade 1972.

Well, there could be that same plaque on the front porch of a lot of homes of a lot of great football players' families in the South (and beyond) that could simply say, "ONLY GOD CAN MAKE A STAR."

Part of what we want to capture in this book is a portion of the "How God Makes Stars."

Experts have said, "Football is a sport in the North, a passion in the Southwest, and a religion in the South."

The authors of this book in one way or another have lived **it**. The lead author has for many years been called to try and illustrate **it** in a book or a movie because **it** is coherently good and close to the heart of God making **it** of a supernatural nature.

What is **it**? **It** is a unique charismatic manner of thinking Deep in the Heart of the American South that incubates, cradles, nurtures, trains, tests, supports, and projects young men, and the passion of their Spirits, into the fullness of their destiny, football or otherwise.

In **its** simplest term, **it** is God-given Star Power, possessed by all of us at various levels. So, as you read this book, just know that the bold **it** is God-given Star Power and feel **it** come to life in this book through various select characters and the UAB football program. You will be surprised and amazed at these Stars of the South, both famous and obscure, but equally bright and powerful and created by God. In this book we are going to show a dynamic relationship between God and football immaculately illustrated through the true story of the history, death, burial, resurrection, return, and future of UAB Football.

The incredible story of UAB Football will most definitely capture your attention. However, the story is much deeper than just UAB Football. Using multiple real-life people and circumstances as visual aids, "Deep in the Heart" Starring UAB Football is about the culture and every unique experience that gives life to greatness in the human spirit in a multitude of ways. "Deep in the Heart" Starring UAB Football is our attempt to capture a unique southern charisma in these stories, but any reader, anywhere can be inspired by this saga. "Deep in the Heart" Starring UAB Football is about what makes a person tick and drives one to greatness in the depths of their spirits.

Much of our story takes place deep in the heart of the American South where four main arteries intersect at the junction of I-65, 59, 22 and 20 in the city of Birmingham, Alabama.

Let's go there now to feel and experience the Spirit that drives the person "Deep in the Heart."

Prologue Devotion

Prologue Worship Song
Michael W. Smith - Vanessa Campagna & Madelyn Berry "Waymaker" Video

Have you, or someone you know, ever believed for something that you couldn't see but it eventually came to pass?

Explain:

What applicable principle can you learn and apply from this observation?

Prayer: *Dear God, Your Word says that "without faith it is impossible to please You." I want to please You, Father,* (Finish writing your own prayer)

_____

_____

Prologue Coaching Point:
You must believe God wants you to exercise your faith.

Chris Hodges Video Message
<u>Running with the Giants Message 1</u>

The Keystone Deep in the Heart Verse:

"And without faith it is impossible to please God, because anyone who comes to him must believe that he exists and that he rewards those who earnestly seek him." (Hebrews 11:6)

Southern Culture and Stars

Lift up your eyes and look to the heavens: Who created all these? He who brings out the starry host one by one and calls forth each of them by name. Because of his great power and mighty strength, not one of them is missing. (Isaiah 40:26-29)

"7 Bridges Road" Video

A "Southern Culture and Stars" Narrative

Billy Graham observed: "Look up on a starry night, and you will see the majesty and power of an infinite Creator."

On any given weekend, look online, on TV, live in a stadium, or on a football field somewhere, you can likewise see the majesty and power of an infinite Creator who loves to watch His children play.

Love it or hate it. Hug its neck or bless its heart. No matter what you think of it, Southern culture is definitely diversely, and furthermore, just plain different. That difference was born and raised in a crowded hothouse full of characters and charisma. Good-hearted people live here, fearfully and wonderfully made, so many of them with distinct stories worth telling.

This book tells the stories of an especially compelling slice of this population that engages so many others. It's all about college football players and coaches and the people, so many people, who care about them so deeply. The sport wasn't invented here, but it found its true home in this rich soil.

The influence of those players and coaches stretches well beyond the mammoth stadiums they entertain. More than in any other part of the country, they inspire a form of worship even among Christians who believe in the one true God.

That's the power of college football in the Deep South, where lines are drawn and lessons learned, players become stars, coaches grow into legends, and game days are holy days year after year after year. Put in the proper perspective, that Southern passion has a purpose and a place. This book will take you there.

"Man travels hundreds of miles to gaze at the broad expanse of the ocean. He looks in awe at the heavens above. He stares in wonderment at the fields, the mountains, the rivers and the streams. And then he passes himself by without a thought-God's most amazing creation."
-**St. Augustine** (399 A.D. paraphrased)

Let's not just pass these amazing people and stories by without a thought. As we take this journey, I will provide for you background documentary sources for each step of the way. Like this:

Documentary
"Holy Day in the Deep South"

Chapter 1 Worship Song
"So Will I (100 BillionX)" - Hillsong United Video

Have you, or someone that you know, ever looked in awe at some facet of God's creation?

Explain.

What applicable principle can you learn and apply from this observation?

(Throughout this book, each chapter will have a Devotional Moment with a prayer and a space for you to write your own prayer followed by a Coaching Point then a video message from a southern pastor.)

Prayer: *Dear God, I worship You, the Creator and appreciate immensely Your creation, especially Your people...Father,*

_____

_____

_____

Lesson 1 Coaching Point:
You must believe God is The Creator and worship Him.

Joel Osteen Video Message
"It's Already Set Up"

Read Proverbs 1 (NIV) and highlight the phrases that speak to your heart:

The proverbs of Solomon son of David, king of Israel: for gaining wisdom and instruction; for understanding words of insight; for receiving instruction in prudent behavior, doing what is right and just and fair; for giving prudence to those who are simple, knowledge and discretion to the young-let the wise listen and add to their learning, and let the discerning get guidance-for understanding proverbs and parables, the sayings and riddles of the wise. The fear of the LORD is the beginning of knowledge, but fools despise wisdom and instruction. Listen, my son, to your father's instruction and do not forsake your mother's teaching. They are a garland to grace your head and a chain to adorn your neck. My son, if sinful men entice you, do not give in to them. If they say, "Come along with us; let's lie in wait for innocent blood, let's ambush some harmless soul; let's swallow them alive, like the grave, and whole, like those who go down to the pit; we will get all sorts of valuable things and fill our houses with plunder; cast lots with us; we will all share the loot"-my son, do not go along with them, do not set foot on their paths; for their feet rush into evil, they are swift to shed blood. How useless to spread a net where every bird can see it! These men lie in wait for their own blood; they ambush only themselves! Such are the paths of all who go after ill-gotten gain; it takes away the life of those who get it. Out in the open wisdom calls aloud, she raises her voice in the public square; on top of the wall she cries out, at the city gate she makes her speech: "How long will you who are simple love your simple ways? How long will mockers delight in mockery and fools hate knowledge? Repent at my rebuke! Then I will pour out my thoughts to you, I will make known to you my teachings. But since you refuse to listen when I call and no one pays attention when I stretch out my hand, since you disregard all my advice and do not accept my rebuke, I in turn will laugh when disaster strikes you; I will mock when calamity overtakes you-when calamity overtakes you like a storm, when disaster sweeps over you like a whirlwind, when distress and trouble overwhelm you. Then they will call to me but I will not answer; they will look for me but will not find me, since they hated knowledge and did not choose to fear the LORD. Since they would not accept my advice and spurned my rebuke, they will eat the fruit of their ways and be filled with the fruit of their schemes. For the waywardness of the simple will kill them, and the complacency of fools will destroy them; but whoever listens to me will live in safety and be at ease, without fear of harm." (Proverbs 1)

The University of the South Legendary Train Ride

He only is my rock and my salvation: he is my defense; I shall not be moved. (Psalm 62:6 KJV)

"Sewanee Story" Video

"The University of the South Legendary Train Ride" Narrative

If you went searching for the heart of college football in the South today, Sewanee, Tennessee is the last place you might look. It's the home of the University of the South, a private Division III university that doesn't award athletic scholarships.

However, more than a century ago, that small school in that small town produced a team for the ages.

It wasn't just that the 1899 Sewanee Tigers went undefeated, untied, and unscored upon except by one opponent, John Heisman's Auburn Tigers, in an 11-10 Sewanee victory. That 12-0 team, with a roster of only twenty-one players, a student manager, a young coach, and an unsung hero - an African-American who may have been the first, (football only), athletic trainer in history, became legendary by completing a road trip that has never been matched and never will be.

In what would be an epic season today, those young men played five games in six days away from home and won each of those games by shutout. They traveled 2,500 miles by train to beat Texas in Austin, Texas A&M in Houston, Tulane in New Orleans, LSU in Baton Rouge, and Ole Miss in Memphis-all in a single week.

It was David taking down Goliath on repeat.

Three decades later, Sewanee would become a charter member of the Southeastern Conference, only to discover it could no longer compete at that level, but its place in the fabric of college football was secure. Any historical discussion of passion and toughness, two of the sport's enduring traits, has to begin with the Iron Men of Sewanee.

Documentary

"Can't Repeat the 1899 Sewanee Iron Men"

"The University of the South Legendary Train Ride"

Chapter 2 Worship Song
Josh Turner - "Long Black Train" Video

Have you, or someone that you know, ever accomplished something that seemed virtually impossible?

Explain.

What applicable principle can you learn and apply from this observation?

Prayer: *Dear God, if You ordain something then nothing in this world can stop that something from happening...Father,*

_____

_____

_____

Lesson 2 Coaching Point:
You must believe God is on your side.

TD Jakes Video Message
"Defying The Urge To Quit"

Read Proverbs 2 (NIV) and highlight the phrases that speak to your heart:

My son, if you accept my words and store up my commands within you, turning your ear to wisdom and applying your heart to understanding-indeed, if you call out for insight and cry aloud for understanding, and if you look for it as for silver and search for it as for hidden treasure, then you will understand the fear of the LORD and find the knowledge of God. For the LORD gives wisdom; from his mouth come knowledge and understanding. He holds success in store for the upright, he is a shield to those whose walk is blameless, for he guards the course of the just and protects the way of his faithful ones. Then you will understand what is right and just and fair-every good path. For wisdom will enter your heart, and knowledge will be pleasant to your soul. Discretion will protect you, and understanding will guard you. Wisdom will save you from the ways of wicked men, from men whose words are perverse, who have left the straight paths to walk in dark ways, who delight in doing wrong and rejoice in the perverseness of evil, whose paths are crooked and who are devious in their ways. Wisdom will save you also from the adulterous woman, from the wayward woman with her seductive words, who has left the partner of her youth and ignored the covenant she made before God. Surely her house leads down to death and her paths to the spirits of the dead. None who go to her return or attain the paths of life. Thus you will walk in the ways of the good and keep to the paths of the righteous. For the upright will live in the land, and the blameless will remain in it; but the wicked will be cut off from the land, and the unfaithful will be torn from it.

John Heisman-Auburn-Clemson-Georgia Tech History

We have this hope as an anchor for the soul, firm and secure. It enters the inner sanctuary behind the curtain, where our forerunner, Jesus, has entered on our behalf. He has become a high priest forever, in the order of Melchizedek. (Hebrews 6:19-20)

"John Heisman-Auburn-Clemson-Georgia Tech History" Video

"John Heisman-Auburn-Clemson-Georgia Tech History" Narrative

Y ou know the name, of course, because it's attached to the most famous trophy in college football, maybe in all of sports. You probably don't know the Heisman Trophy's namesake because his role in cultivating the sport in the South began in the late 1800s.

John Heisman was a carpetbagger of sorts, born in Ohio, schooled as player and coach north of the Mason-Dixon line, but he left such a legacy in his adopted part of the country he was dubbed "the pioneer of Southern football."

His reputation began from humble seeds during a brief stay away from the game. When Auburn reached out in search of a coach, he was working at a tomato farm in Marshall, Texas. Rediscovering his true calling, he would help grow three Southern football powers in Auburn, Clemson, and Georgia Tech. His last Auburn team in 1899 was the only opponent to score on the legendary Iron Men of Sewanee.

Heisman was a true innovator with a fertile mind. Among his many lasting contributions to the game, he was credited with promoting legalization of the forward pass, having a quarterback call out cadence at the line and popularizing the notion of the football coach as, in his words, "little short of a czar." His hard-nosed attitude was reflected in one of his more memorable phrases: "Gentlemen, it is better to have died as a small boy than to fumble this football."

That spirit lives on in more than the trophy that bears his name. It lives on with the strongest heartbeat in the Deep South.

Documentary

"John Heisman: The Man Behind the Award and His Time at Clemson"

"John Heisman-Auburn-Clemson-Georgia-Tech History"

Chapter 3 Worship Song

Ray Boltz "The Anchor Holds" Video

Have you, or someone you know, ever hoped for something phenomenal and the hope kept you moving forward during difficult times?

Explain.

What applicable principle can you learn and apply from this observation?

Prayer: *Dear God, hope in You anchors my soul, gives me hope for the future and power in the present...Father,*

_____

_____

_____

Lesson 3 Coaching Point:

You must believe God is providing your hope in Jesus.

Craig Groeschel Video Message
"Seed Of Faith"

Read Proverbs 3 (NIV) and highlight the phrases that speak to your heart:

My son, do not forget my teaching, but keep my commands in your heart, for they will prolong your life many years and bring you peace and prosperity. Let love and faithfulness never leave you; bind them around your neck, write them on the tablet of your heart. Then you will win favor and a good name in the sight of God and man. Trust in the LORD with all your heart and lean not on your own understanding; in all your ways submit to him, and he will make your paths straight. Do not be wise in your own eyes; fear the LORD and shun evil. This will bring health to your body and nourishment to your bones. Honor the LORD with your wealth, with the first fruits of all your crops; then your barns will be filled to overflowing, and your vats will brim over with new wine. My son, do not despise the LORD's discipline, and do not resent his rebuke, because the LORD disciplines those he loves, as a father the son he delights in. Blessed are those who find wisdom, those who gain understanding, for she is more profitable than silver and yields better returns than gold. She is more precious than rubies; nothing you desire can compare with her. Long life is in her right hand; in her left hand are riches and honor. Her ways are pleasant ways, and all her paths are peace. She is a tree of life to those who take hold of her; those who hold her fast will be blessed. By wisdom the LORD laid the earth's foundations, by understanding he set the heavens in place; by his knowledge the watery depths were divided, and the clouds let drop the dew. My son, do not let wisdom and understanding out of your sight, preserve sound judgment and discretion; they will be life for you, an ornament to grace your neck. Then you will go on your way in safety, and your foot will not stumble. When you lie down, you will not be afraid; when you lie down, your sleep will be sweet. Have no fear of sudden disaster or of the ruin that overtakes the wicked, for the LORD will be at your side and will keep your foot from being snared. Do not withhold good from those to whom it is due, when it is in your power to act. Do not say to your neighbor, "Come back tomorrow and I'll give it to you"-when you already have it with you. Do not plot harm against your neighbor, who lives trustfully near you. Do not accuse anyone for no reason-when they have done you no harm. Do not envy the violent or choose any of their ways. For the LORD detests the perverse but takes the upright into his confidence. The LORD's curse is on the house of the wicked, but he blesses the home of the righteous. He mocks proud mockers but shows favor to the humble and oppressed. The wise inherit honor, but fools get only shame. (Proverbs 3)

Birmingham and Legion Field: The Epicenter for This Way of Life

Do not be deceived: God cannot be mocked. A man reaps what he sows. Whoever sows to please their flesh, from the flesh will reap destruction; whoever sows to please the Spirit, from the Spirit will reap eternal life. Let us not become weary in doing good, for at the proper time we will reap a harvest if we do not give up. (Galatians 6:7-9)

"Southern Man" SEC Highlights Video

"The Epicenter for This Way of Life" Narrative

Walk inside Legion Field, which once proudly splashed Birmingham's designation as "Football Capital of the South" across its facade, and you can feel the history. If steel and concrete could talk, imagine the stories the Gray Lady on Graymont could tell in her ninth decade of service.

Legion Field has been the primary home of two Division I programs (UAB and Alabama), the best rivalry game in the country (the Iron Bowl between Alabama and Auburn), the largest HBCU Classic in the country (the Magic City Classic between Alabama A&M and Alabama State), two conference championship games (SEC and SWAC) and four bowl games (Dixie, Hall of Fame, All-American, and Birmingham).

And that's just the college football highlights. Legion Field also has been home to eight professional teams, two NFL preseason games, one AFL regular-season game as well as the Alabama High School Athletic Association state championships.

The passion for football burns so bright here that for the past seventeen consecutive years, for college football games televised by ESPN, Birmingham has been the No. 1 local market, and oh yeah, the headquarters for the SEC.

The sport stirs Birmingham's blood like no other because the qualities football demands and rewards-toughness, grit, mettle-live deep in the city's soil. Like its namesake in England, the largest city in Alabama was forged on the iron and steel industry.

The American Birmingham boomed so quickly it became known as "The Magic City."

Young men have made magic in the SEC and at Legion Field in Birmingham since 1927. They still do. It remains a special place to play football and to watch football because no place cares about football more.

Documentary

"The Football Capital of the South"

"The Epicenter for This Way of Life"

Chapter 4 Worship Song
Blake Shelton "God's Country"

What seed have you, or someone you know, planted in life and witnessed the greatest harvest from?

Explain.

What applicable principle can you learn and apply from this observation?

Prayer: *Dear God you created the seed, time and harvest principle and it always applies...Father,*

_____

_____

_____

Lesson 4 Coaching Point:
You must believe God has a process of spiritual agriculture.

Joel Osteen Video Message

"The Power Of The Soil"

Read Proverbs 4 (NIV) and highlight the phrases that speak to your heart:

Listen, my sons, to a father's instruction; pay attention and gain understanding. I give you sound learning, so do not forsake my teaching. For I too was a son to my father, still tender, and cherished by my mother. Then he taught me, and he said to me, "Take hold of my words with all your heart; keep my commands, and you will live. Get wisdom, get understanding; do not forget my words or turn away from them. Do not forsake wisdom, and she will protect you; love her, and she will watch over you. The beginning of wisdom is this: Get wisdom. Though it cost all you have, get understanding. Cherish her, and she will exalt you; embrace her, and she will honor you. She will give you a garland to grace your head and present you with a glorious crown." Listen, my son, accept what I say, and the years of your life will be many. I instruct you in the way of wisdom and lead you along straight paths. When you walk, your steps will not be hampered; when you run, you will not stumble. Hold on to instruction, do not let it go; guard it well, for it is your life. Do not set foot on the path of the wicked or walk in the way of evildoers. Avoid it, do not travel on it; turn from it and go on your way. For they cannot rest until they do evil; they are robbed of sleep till they make someone stumble. They eat the bread of wickedness and drink the wine of violence. The path of the righteous is like the morning sun, shining ever brighter till the full light of day. But the way of the wicked is like deep darkness; they do not know what makes them stumble. My son, pay attention to what I say; turn your ear to my words. Do not let them out of your sight, keep them within your heart; for they are life to those who find them and health to one's whole body. Above all else, guard your heart, for everything you do flows from it. Keep your mouth free of perversity; keep corrupt talk far from your lips. Let your eyes look straight ahead; fix your gaze directly before you. Give careful thought to the paths for your feet and be steadfast in all your ways. Do not turn to the right or the left; keep your foot from evil.

Chapter 5

Roots of UAB Athletics

Therefore, since we are surrounded by such a great cloud of witnesses, let us throw off everything that hinders and the sin that so easily entangles. And let us run with perseverance the race marked out for us. (Hebrews 12:1)

Gene Bartow Tribute Video

"Roots of UAB Athletics" Narrative

UAB's first president, Dr. Joseph F. Volker, set the tone for what the University of Alabama at Birmingham could and would become when he said, "We would do Birmingham a great disservice if we dream too little dreams."

Volker's successor, Dr. S. Richardson Hill Jr., put that philosophy in action in a big way in 1977 when he hired Gene Bartow away from UCLA as athletics director and head basketball coach.

It was the upset of the decade in that sport.

UAB didn't yet have a basketball team, and the university lived deep in the heart of football country. Bartow was so highly regarded that UCLA had chosen him to succeed the legendary John Wooden, and he'd led the Bruins to the Final Four just as he had the Memphis State Tigers.

Defying conventional wisdom, Bartow took the road less traveled to build something from nothing in Birmingham. He chose UAB over UCLA, and that made all the difference in laying the foundation for a fully functioning Division I athletics program. UAB and Bartow became the perfect marriage of an institution and a leader with big dreams.

Those dreams started with basketball. Because Bartow was a visionary who saw the big picture, football was sure to follow.

Documentary: "Farewell to a Legend"

"Roots of UAB Athletics"

Chapter 5 Worship Song

Nicole C. Mullen - "My Redeemer Lives"

What legendary person have you, or someone you know, admired and why?

Explain.

What applicable principle can you learn and apply from this observation?

Prayer: *Dear God your gift to me is my talent and my gift to You is how I use it. To whom much is given, much is expected...Father,*

_____

_____

_____

Lesson 5 Coaching Point:

You must believe God has witnesses cheering you on.

Steven Furtick Video Message
"Don't Waste Your Angel"

Read Proverbs 5 (NIV) and highlight the phrases that speak to your heart:

My son, pay attention to my wisdom, turn your ear to my words of insight, that you may maintain discretion and your lips may preserve knowledge. For the lips of the adulterous woman drip honey, and her speech is smoother than oil; but in the end she is bitter as gall, sharp as a double-edged sword. Her feet go down to death; her steps lead straight to the grave. She gives no thought to the way of life; her paths wander aimlessly, but she does not know it. Now then, my sons, listen to me; do not turn aside from what I say. Keep to a path far from her, do not go near the door of her house, lest you lose your honor to others and your dignity to one who is cruel, lest strangers feast on your wealth and your toil enrich the house of another. At the end of your life you will groan, when your flesh and body are spent. You will say, "How I hated discipline! How my heart spurned correction! I would not obey my teachers or turn my ear to my instructors. And I was soon in serious trouble in the assembly of God's people." Drink water from your own cistern, running water from your own well. Should your springs overflow in the streets, your streams of water in the public squares? Let them be yours alone, never to be shared with strangers. May your fountain be blessed, and may you rejoice in the wife of your youth. A loving doe, a graceful deer-may her breasts satisfy you always, may you ever be intoxicated with her love. Why, my son, be intoxicated with another man's wife? Why embrace the bosom of a wayward woman? For your ways are in full view of the LORD, and he examines all your paths. The evil deeds of the wicked ensnare them; the cords of their sins hold them fast. For lack of discipline they will die, led astray by their own great folly.

Chapter 6

Bear Bryant and Eddie Robinson Types

Do not withhold discipline from a child; if you punish them with the rod, they will not die. (Proverbs 23:13)

Bear Bryant Teaching Video

Eddie Robinson Video

"Bear Bryant and Eddie Robinson Types" Narrative

N o matter how special they are, the players come and go, but one thing remains that sets college football apart: *the coaches and the very best ones come to define their programs and their sport.*

No two coaches epitomize the sport of college football for generations of young men in the Deep South, where it matters most, quite like Arkansas native Paul "Bear" Bryant and Louisiana's Eddie Robinson.

Bryant was a winner at Maryland, Kentucky and Texas A&M. He became a larger-than-life legend when he answered Mama's call to return home to his alma mater, Alabama. Bryant won a record six national championships with the Crimson Tide, and his influence resonates to this day beyond the scoreboard decades after his final victory. His growling voice echoes from the loudspeakers in the stadium that bears his name, where houndstooth clothing, patterned after his signature hat, is the look of choice.

Down on that sideline, a modern-day Bear has emerged in Alabama coach Nick Saban, matching Bryant's six national titles, preaching the same old-school values of toughness, accountability, and teamwork. Like the memory of the Bear, those values remain embedded deep in the heart of the game.

Over in Louisiana, few if any have had greater impact on the lives and the culture through the game of football as has the legendary Eddie Robinson. Coach Robinson became the first coach to record 400 wins thus becoming recognized as the "winningest coach in college football history," Robinson ultimately recorded 408 wins. Over 200 of Coach Robinson's former players went on to play in the NFL including his successor at Grambling and Super Bowl MVP Doug Williams.

Coach Robinson once said, "The most important thing in football is the boy who plays the game, you can't coach 'em unless you love 'em." He loved them and they rose to the occasion because of it.

Documentaries

"Bear Bryant 'simply the best there ever was'"

"Grambling's Eddie Robinson: Molding Men"

Bear Bryant and Eddie Robinson Types"

Chapter 6 Worship Song
Chris Tomlin - Pat Barrett "Good Good Father"

Can you site an example of when doing something hard led to helping you, or someone that you know, accomplish a goal? Explain.

What applicable principle can you learn and apply from this observation?

Prayer: *Dear God, if I discipline myself to do the things that I need to do when I need to do them then the day will come when I will be able to do the things that I want to do when I want to do them...Father,*

_____

_____

_____

Lesson 6 Coaching Point:
You must believe God requires discipline for you to succeed.

Steven Furtick Video Message
"God Will Fulfill His Purpose For You"

Read Proverbs 6 (NIV) and highlight the phrases that speak to your heart:

My son, if you have put up security for your neighbor, if you have shaken hands in pledge for a stranger, you have been trapped by what you said, ensnared by the words of your mouth. So do this, my son, to free yourself, since you have fallen into your neighbor's hands: Go-to the point of exhaustion-and give your neighbor no rest! Allow no sleep to your eyes, no slumber to your eyelids. Free yourself, like a gazelle from the hand of the hunter, like a bird from the snare of the fowler. Go to the ant, you sluggard; consider its ways and be wise! It has no commander, no overseer or ruler, yet it stores its provisions in summer and gathers its food at harvest. How long will you lie there, you sluggard? When will you get up from your sleep? A little sleep, a little slumber, a little folding of the hands to rest-and poverty will come on you like a thief and scarcity like an armed man. A troublemaker and a villain, who goes about with a corrupt mouth, who winks maliciously with his eye, signals with his feet and motions with his fingers, who plots evil with deceit in his heart-he always stirs up conflict. Therefore disaster will overtake him in an instant; he will suddenly be destroyed-without remedy. There are six things the LORD hates, seven that are detestable to him: haughty eyes, a lying tongue, hands that shed innocent blood, a heart that devises wicked schemes, feet that are quick to rush into evil, a false witness who pours out lies and a person who stirs up conflict in the community. My son, keep your father's command and do not forsake your mother's teaching. Bind them always on your heart; fasten them around your neck. When you walk, they will guide you; when you sleep, they will watch over you; when you awake, they will speak to you. For this command is a lamp, this teaching is a light and correction and instruction are the way to life, keeping you from your neighbor's wife, from the smooth talk of a wayward woman. Do not lust in your heart after her beauty or let her captivate you with her eyes. For a prostitute can be had for a loaf of bread, but another man's wife preys on your very life. Can a man scoop fire into his lap without his clothes being burned? Can a man walk on hot coals without his feet being scorched? So is he who sleeps with another man's wife; no one who touches her will go unpunished. People do not despise a thief if he steals to satisfy his hunger when he is starving. Yet if he is caught, he must pay sevenfold, though it costs him all the wealth of his house. But a man who commits adultery has no sense; whoever does so destroys himself. Blows and disgrace are his lot, and his shame will never be wiped away. For jealousy arouses a husband's fury, and he will show no mercy when he takes revenge. He will not accept any compensation; he will refuse a bribe, however great it is.

Chapter 7

The Iron Bowl and Legion Field Legendary

Do you think I cannot call on my Father, and he will at once put at my disposal more than twelve legions of angels? But how then would the Scriptures be fulfilled that say it must happen in this way?" (Matthew 26:53-54)

Iron Bowl Kick 6 Video

"The Iron Bowl and Legion Field Legendary" Narrative

Alabama vs. Auburn at Legion Field in Birmingham was never just another football game in just another football stadium. It was a game that stirred the blood of an entire state with an unsurpassed passion for the sport. It was played in the state's biggest stadium in its largest city, an industrial city with iron ore in its soil and steel at its heart. The tickets and the passion were divided in half so that every play sparked roars of approval and dissent.

It was a game that demanded its own name, and legendary Auburn coach Shug Jordan provided it. He called it simply the Iron Bowl.

No other annual college rivalry has witnessed as many legendary players, coaches, teams, plays, and games in such an iconic setting. Bear Bryant became college football's all-time winningest coach when Alabama came from behind to capture the 1981 Iron Bowl. The next year, Auburn ended a record nine-game losing streak in the rivalry on freshman running back Bo Jackson's twisting dive, aka Bo Over the Top.

Those unforgettable moments were captured in paintings that still hang on living room walls from Huntsville to Mobile, in stories passed down through generations.

Football matters in Alabama in a way you have to experience to understand. For one Saturday in November, one game in particular matters unlike any other to the entire state. It's played now on campus in Tuscaloosa and Auburn, and it's still called the Iron

Bowl, but the old-timers will quickly set you straight. It never mattered more than when it was played at Legion Field.

When you walk through those gates on to Legion Field to this day you can feel the hallowed past and breathe the greatness of historic Iron Bowls as well as other epic games played at The Old Gray Lady in The Magic City.

Documentary

"Legion Field's Greatest Games"

"The Iron Bowl and Legion Field Legendary"

Chapter 7 Worship Song

Michael W. Smith "Breathe"

Can you site an example of feeling like supernatural forces are working on behalf of you or someone that you know?

Explain.

What applicable principle can you learn and apply from this observation?

Prayer: *Dear God the powers that are for me are much greater than the powers that are against me...Father,*

_____

_____

_____

Lesson 7 Coaching Point:

You must believe God has angels working on your behalf.

Joel Osteen Video Message
<u>"It's The Heart That Matters"</u>

Read Proverbs 7 (NIV) and highlight the phrases that speak to your heart:

My son, keep my words and store up my commands within you. Keep my commands and you will live; guard my teachings as the apple of your eye. Bind them on your fingers; write them on the tablet of your heart. Say to wisdom, "You are my sister," and to insight, "You are my relative." They will keep you from the adulterous woman, from the wayward woman with her seductive words. At the window of my house I looked down through the lattice. I saw among the simple, I noticed among the young men, a youth who had no sense. He was going down the street near her corner, walking along in the direction of her house at twilight, as the day was fading, as the dark of night set in. Then out came a woman to meet him, dressed like a prostitute and with crafty intent. (She is unruly and defiant, her feet never stay at home; now in the street, now in the squares, at every corner she lurks.) She took hold of him and kissed him and with a brazen face she said: "Today I fulfilled my vows, and I have food from my fellowship offering at home. So I came out to meet you; I looked for you and have found you! I have covered my bed with colored linens from Egypt. I have perfumed my bed with myrrh, aloes and cinnamon. Come, let's drink deeply of love till morning; let's enjoy ourselves with love! My husband is not at home; he has gone on a long journey. He took his purse filled with money and will not be home till full moon." With persuasive words she led him astray; she seduced him with her smooth talk. All at once he followed her like an ox going to the slaughter, like a deer stepping into a noose till an arrow pierces his liver, like a bird darting into a snare, little knowing it will cost him his life. Now then, my sons, listen to me; pay attention to what I say. Do not let your heart turn to her ways or stray into her paths. Many are the victims she has brought down; her slain are a mighty throng. Her house is a highway to the grave, leading down to the chambers of death.

Chapter 8

Roots of UAB Football

Being confident of this, that he who began a good work in you will carry it on to completion until the day of Christ Jesus. (Philippians 1:6)

Derrick Holden: "Football is the Game of Life"

"Roots of UAB Football" Narrative

It started with faith and hope and not much more. They taped ankles in the back of pickup trucks. They practiced on a field better suited as a stand-in for the lunar surface. They endured one hardship after another because Gene Bartow was more than the coach starting a UAB basketball program. He was the athletics director who understood something about his new home in Birmingham.

Football is deep in the heart of the American South. Even as he was leading the Blazers to the NCAA Tournament's Sweet 16 and Elite Eight early in his tenure, Bartow knew adding a football program was essential to the long-term health of UAB athletics. He tapped Dr. Jim Hilyer, a veteran coach with college and professional experience who was teaching at UAB, to launch the effort in 1989.

Unlike all other teams at UAB, the football team would not be called Blazers. Instead, they would be called Lasers and would be a club team until all requirements to be an official NCAA program were met. The Lasers would practice on the Intramural field, but it was not available until 8 P.M. as the women's flag football teams were still playing. There was no equipment; it had been ordered but was not in yet. The training room would not be available for the Lasers, but the Lasers did have a trainer assigned to them. The trainer had a pickup truck and had agreed to work the practices out of his pickup truck. One game had been scheduled for the first Saturday in September.

The first task was to see if enough students were interested in playing to field a team. Fliers were placed in all classrooms and other places where students might see them. At the posted time, 105 students showed up eager to play. Forms were filled out and students were told to return the next evening at 8 P.M. in shorts, T-shirts, and sneakers. Hilyer contacted some ex-players that he thought would be good coaches. By the next evening at 8 P.M., a staff of six coaches were present. UAB Football was born.

Practice was held in shorts and T-shirts until the first scheduled game. The equipment had not yet arrived so Hilyer cancelled the game. Hilyer had scheduled later games with Marion Institute, Samford Junior Varsity, and Miles College. By the day of the first game with Marion Institute, the equipment was in, the team number was down to sixty-five, and the coaching staff was up to eight. That first season the Lasers played six games, each team twice. The Lasers record was 0-6. Progress was measured by scores from the first game compared with the score of the second game with the same team.

The second season, the Lasers played eight games and finished with a 4-4 record. During the club team's two seasons, there were many unusual situations. Any student enrolled in UAB was eligible to play on the club team. The quarterback for the first season was a medical student and several graduate students played at various times. Some of the first-year club team players had not even played football in high school, which resulted in many funny stories.

The day after the first game with Samford in the first year, Coach Bartow called and asked Hilyer to stop by his office. Bartow told Hilyer that some of his players had caused a problem in a bar after the game. Hilyer asked how they knew they were UAB players. Bartow replied that the players still had on their uniforms! Another incident occurred when a player left his cleats at home and had to play in his high-top work boots. The beginnings of UAB football were not impressive but paved the way for the future.

After the second year of the club team, UAB met the NCAA criteria and became a Division 3 team. At that time, NCAA rules allowed a school to have mixed division teams. All UAB sports were Division 1 except football. UAB played two seasons as a Division 3 team. Both years were winning seasons for the Blazers.

Hilyer lifted the Blazers from club program to Division III to Division I-AA in a mere five years, setting the stage for the leap to Division I-A.

All these years later, Hilyer still contributes to the program as a volunteer, adding his administrative and mental training expertise.

UAB football started with a leap of faith. Bartow believed in football and he believed in the humble Hilyer. That faith has been rewarded.

Documentary

"UAB Blazer Football History"

"Roots of UAB Football"

Chapter 8 Worship Song
Hillsong Worship "What a Beautiful Name"

Can you site a time in your life, or the life of someone you know, that started something, and it took longer than expected to finish but it did get finished well?

Explain.

What applicable principle can you learn and apply from this observation?

Prayer: *Dear God You always finish what You start...Father,*

_____

_____

_____

Lesson 8 Coaching Point:
You must believe God finishes what he began.

Steven Furtick Video Message

Steven Furtick Video Message
<u>"Expect Something Great"</u>

Read Proverbs 8 (NIV) and highlight the phrases that speak to your heart:

Does not wisdom call out? Does not understanding raise her voice? At the highest point along the way, where the paths meet, she takes her stand; beside the gate leading into the city, at the entrance, she cries aloud: "To you, O people, I call out; I raise my voice to all mankind. You who are simple, gain prudence; you who are foolish, set your hearts on it. Listen, for I have trustworthy things to say; I open my lips to speak what is right. My mouth speaks what is true, for my lips detest wickedness. All the words of my mouth are just; none of them is crooked or perverse. To the discerning all of them are right; they are upright to those who have found knowledge. Choose my instruction instead of silver, knowledge rather than choice gold, for wisdom is more precious than rubies, and nothing you desire can compare with her. "I, wisdom, dwell together with prudence; I possess knowledge and discretion. To fear the LORD is to hate evil; I hate pride and arrogance, evil behavior and perverse speech. Counsel and sound judgment are mine; I have insight, I have power. By me kings reign and rulers issue decrees that are just; by me princes govern, and nobles-all who rule on earth. I love those who love me, and those who seek me find me. With me are riches and honor, enduring wealth and prosperity. My fruit is better than fine gold; what I yield surpasses choice silver. I walk in the way of righteousness, along the paths of justice, bestowing a rich inheritance on those who love me and making their treasuries full. "The LORD brought me forth as the first of his works, before his deeds of old; I was formed long ages ago, at the very beginning, when the world came to be. When there were no watery depths, I was given birth, when there were no springs overflowing with water; before the mountains were settled in place, before the hills, I was given birth, before he made the world or its fields or any of the dust of the earth. I was there when he set the heavens in place, when he marked out the horizon on the face of the deep, when he estab- lished the clouds above and fixed securely the fountains of the deep, when he gave the sea its boundary so the waters would not overstep his command, and when he marked out the foundations of the earth. Then I was constantly at his side. I was filled with delight day after day, rejoicing always in his presence, rejoicing in his whole world and delighting in mankind. "Now then, my children, listen to me; blessed are those who keep my ways. Listen to my instruction and be wise; do not disregard it. Blessed are those who listen to me, watching daily at my doors,

waiting at my doorway. For those who find me find life and receive favor from the LORD. But those who fail to find me harm themselves; all who hate me love death."
(Proverbs 8)

A Little Bit of Blazer History

All those gathered here will know that it is not by sword or spear that the LORD saves; for the battle is the LORD's, and he will give all of you into our hands." (1 Samuel 17:47)

Dooley Remembers Video

"A Little Bit of History" Narrative

Watson Brown took over for Dr. Jim Hilyer to take UAB football to the next level, and the veteran Brown delivered encouraging glimpses of promise during his 12-year tenure.

The first win over a ranked team against No. 18 East Carolina in 1999. The first winning season in Division I-A in 2000. The first bowl trip in 2004, a season that featured victories over Mississippi State from the SEC and future Big 12 powers Baylor and TCU.

No game showed what was possible quite like the 2000 road trip to LSU. The Blazers, who live in the heart of SEC country, scored their first victory over an SEC program in no less a hostile environment than Death Valley in Baton Rouge.

That win would gain significance over time because the LSU coach, in his first year with the Tigers, was Nick Saban. After the game, a despondent Saban told a friend, "I don't know if I can win here."

People have wondered the same thing about UAB football since its birth as the head coaching baton passed from Hilyer to Brown to Neil Callaway to Garrick McGee. Brown in particular gave UAB fans reasons to believe, but the Blazers wouldn't fully deliver on their promise until the arrival of Bill Clark.

Documentary

"Looking Back at Notable Moments in UAB Football History"

"A Little Bit of History"

Chapter 9 Worship Song
<u>Hillsong "Mighty To Save"</u>

Do you, or someone you know, have a David and Goliath story where extraordinary odds were overcome for a victory?

Explain.

What applicable principle can you learn and apply from this observation?

Prayer: *Dear God there are times when all odds may be against me, but these are the times when You are able to show Yourself strong...Father,*

_____

_____

_____

Lesson 9 Coaching Point:

You must believe God on your side assures you that you will always win in the end.

TD Jakes Video Message
"Destiny From The Perspective Of Focus"

Read Proverbs 9 (NIV) and highlight the phrases that speak to your heart:

Wisdom has built her house; she has set up its seven pillars. She has prepared her meat and mixed her wine; she has also set her table. She has sent out her servants, and she calls from the highest point of the city, "Let all who are simple come to my house!" To those who have no sense she says, "Come, eat my food and drink the wine I have mixed. Leave your simple ways and you will live; walk in the way of insight." Whoever corrects a mocker invites insults; whoever rebukes the wicked incurs abuse. Do not rebuke mockers or they will hate you; rebuke the wise and they will love you. Instruct the wise and they will be wiser still; teach the righteous and they will add to their learning. The fear of the LORD is the beginning of wisdom, and knowledge of the Holy One is understanding. For through wisdom your days will be many, and years will be added to your life. If you are wise, your wisdom will reward you; if you are a mocker, you alone will suffer. Folly is an unruly woman; she is simple and knows nothing. She sits at the door of her house, on a seat at the highest point of the city, calling out to those who pass by, who go straight on their way, "Let all who are simple come to my house!" To those who have no sense she says, "Stolen water is sweet; food eaten in secret is delicious!" But little do they know that the dead are there, that her guests are deep in the realm of the dead. (Proverbs 9)

Chapter 10

Bill Clark

*Praise the LORD. Blessed are those who fear the LORD,
who find great delight in his commands. Their children
will be mighty in the land; the generation of the upright
will be blessed.* (Psalm 112:1-2)

Bill Clark Story Video

"Bill Clark" Narrative

The star of the story is the big-hearted, salt-of-the-earth Bill Clark. He was born to coach football in the state of Alabama, just as his father had for so many years at the high school level. The younger Clark became not just a winner but a total program builder.

He constructed a dynasty in nine years as head coach at Prattville High School, a run that concluded with back-to-back state championships. He then helped build a new program from scratch in five years as defensive coordinator at the University of South Alabama. He took his first college head coaching job at his alma mater, Jacksonville State, where he led the Gamecocks to their first Football Championship Subdivision playoff wins in his first year.

After that season, Clark left familiar ground to take on his biggest challenge as head coach at UAB, a program that had spiraled from losing games to losing hope. In his first year in Birmingham, he quickly began to improve the attitude and the outlook. The Blazers won six games, their highest total in 10 years, as they earned bowl eligibility for the first time in a decade.

As you will see in the chapters to follow, before he could add to that foundation, the program was shut down.

No one would've blamed him had he left to continue coaching elsewhere, but he wasn't built that way. Instead he stayed and he believed. His faith inspired so many others to fight to bring UAB football back. Together, with Clark as the motivating force, they would bring it back better than ever.

Documentary

"What Drives UAB Head Football Coach Bill Clark"

"Bill Clark"

Chapter 10 Worship Song
Zach Williams – "Fear Is a Liar"

Are you, or someone that you know, apparently blessed in large because of a parent?

Explain.

What applicable principle can you learn and apply from this observation?

Prayer: *Dear God I know that faithful parents produce children who do great things...Father,*

_____

_____

_____

Lesson 10 Coaching Point:

You must believe God will bless families of those who fear and delight in Him.

Steven Furtick Video Message
"Fear Or Faith: One Has To Win"

Read Proverbs 10 (NIV) and highlight the phrases that speak to your heart:

The proverbs of Solomon: A wise son brings joy to his father, but a foolish son brings grief to his mother. Ill-gotten treasures have no lasting value, but righteousness delivers from death. The LORD does not let the righteous go hungry, but he thwarts the craving of the wicked. Lazy hands make for poverty, but diligent hands bring wealth. He who gathers crops in summer is a prudent son, but he who sleeps during harvest is a disgraceful son. Blessings crown the head of the righteous, but violence overwhelms the mouth of the wicked. The name of the righteous is used in blessings, but the name of the wicked will rot. The wise in heart accept commands, but a chattering fool comes to ruin. Whoever walks in integrity walks securely, but whoever takes crooked paths will be found out. Whoever winks maliciously causes grief, and a chattering fool comes to ruin. The mouth of the righteous is a fountain of life, but the mouth of the wicked conceals violence. Hatred stirs up conflict, but love covers over all wrongs. Wisdom is found on the lips of the discerning, but a rod is for the back of one who has no sense. The wise store up knowledge, but the mouth of a fool invites ruin. The wealth of the rich is their fortified city, but poverty is the ruin of the poor. The wages of the righteous is life, but the earnings of the wicked are sin and death. Whoever heeds discipline shows the way to life, but whoever ignores correction leads others astray. Whoever conceals hatred with lying lips and spreads slander is a fool. Sin is not ended by multiplying words, but the prudent hold their tongues. The tongue of the righteous is choice silver, but the heart of the wicked is of little value. The lips of the righteous nourish many, but fools die for lack of sense. The blessing of the LORD brings wealth, without painful toil for it. A fool finds pleasure in wicked schemes, but a person of understanding delights in wisdom. What the wicked dread will overtake them; what the righteous desire will be granted. When the storm has swept by, the wicked are gone, but the righteous stand firm forever. As vinegar to the teeth and smoke to the eyes, so are sluggards to those who send them. The fear of the LORD adds length to life, but the years of the wicked are cut short. The prospect of the righteous is joy, but the hopes of the wicked come to nothing. The way of the LORD is a refuge for the blameless, but it is the ruin of those who do evil. The righteous will never be uprooted, but the wicked will not remain in the land. From the mouth of the righteous comes the fruit of wisdom, but a perverse tongue will be silenced. The lips of the righteous know what finds favor, but the mouth of the wicked only what is perverse. (Proverbs 10)

Chapter 11

One Play vs. Marshall

Jesus replied, "You do not realize now what I am doing, but later you will understand." (John 13:7)

Jordan Howard Over the Top Video

"One Play vs. Marshall" Narrative

I t came down to one play for a 2014 UAB football team on the verge of extinction. Which one play was it? Was it the one key special team block that was missed? Was it the one play to make an interception for a TD instead of letting it slip through the Blazer's DB hands into the Marshall receiver's hands for a critical game saving 1st down on a finishing drive for the Thundering Herd?

Was it the one play to gain one yard to make a first down inside the 10-yard line with one minute to play to score the one touchdown that would beat the undefeated and 18th-ranked Marshall Thundering Herd?

One last chance to show the world that the Blazers, in the face of all the questions swirling about their program's future, were worth saving.

Every one of the 28,355 people in Legion Field knew what was coming. Jordan Howard, UAB's workhorse running back who already had carried 38 times for 169 yards and two touchdowns, was coming.

But this one time, Marshall was ready, and the Herd stopped Howard short. The best effort of an underdog football team wasn't enough to stage one of the bigger upsets in school history, and it wasn't enough to change the course of that history.

We will never know which one play it was.

The administration's decision to shut down the UAB football program wouldn't be announced for 10 days, but the decision already was final. That one play vs. Marshall foreshadowed the greater anguish of the entire UAB football family to come.

What the Blazers did against Marshall on November 22, 2014, with the executioner sharpening his blade, was inspiring. On the big scoreboard, in the bigger picture, it was too little, too late.

Documentary

Save UAB football, and scaring teams like Marshall is just the beginning of what program may accomplish.

"One Play vs. Marshall"

Chapter 11 Worship Song

Ryan Stevenson "Eye of the Storm"

Is there anything that you, or someone you know, is not understanding right now?

Explain.

What applicable principle can you learn and apply from this observation?

Prayer: *Dear God you are God and our ways are not Your ways...Father,*

_____

_____

_____

Lesson 11 Coaching Point:

You must believe God has a perfect plan whether you understand it or not.

Craig Groeschel Video Message
<u>"Praying Through The Pain"</u>

Read Proverbs 11 (NIV) and highlight the phrases that speak to your heart:

The LORD detests dishonest scales, but accurate weights find favor with him. When pride comes, then comes disgrace, but with humility comes wisdom. The integrity of the upright guides them, but the unfaithful are destroyed by their duplicity. Wealth is worthless in the day of wrath, but righteousness delivers from death. The righteousness of the blameless makes their paths straight, but the wicked are brought down by their own wickedness. The righteousness of the upright delivers them, but the unfaithful are trapped by evil desires. Hopes placed in mortals die with them; all the promise of their power comes to nothing. The righteous person is rescued from trouble, and it falls on the wicked instead. With their mouths the godless destroy their neighbors, but through knowledge the righteous escape. When the righteous prosper, the city rejoices; when the wicked perish, there are shouts of joy. Through the blessing of the upright a city is exalted, but by the mouth of the wicked it is destroyed. Whoever derides their neighbor has no sense, but the one who has understanding holds their tongue. A gossip betrays a confidence, but a trustworthy person keeps a secret. For lack of guidance a nation falls, but victory is won through many advisers. Whoever puts up security for a stranger will surely suffer, but whoever refuses to shake hands in pledge is safe. A kindhearted woman gains honor, but ruthless men gain only wealth. Those who are kind benefit themselves, but the cruel bring ruin on themselves. A wicked person earns deceptive wages, but the one who sows righteousness reaps a sure reward. Truly the righteous attain life, but whoever pursues evil finds death. The LORD detests those whose hearts are perverse, but he delights in those whose ways are blameless. Be sure of this: The wicked will not go unpunished, but those who are righteous will go free. Like a gold ring in a pig's snout is a beautiful woman who shows no discretion. The desire of the righteous ends only in good, but the hope of the wicked only in wrath. One person gives freely, yet gains even more; another withholds unduly, but comes to poverty. A generous person will prosper; whoever refreshes others will be refreshed. People curse the one who hoards grain, but they pray God's blessing on the one who is willing to sell. Whoever seeks good finds favor, but evil comes to one who searches for it. Those who trust in their riches will fall, but the righteous will thrive like a green leaf. Whoever brings ruin on their family will inherit only wind, and the fool will be servant to the wise. The fruit of the righteous is a tree of life, and the one who is wise saves lives. If the righteous receive their due on earth, how much more the ungodly and the sinner! (Proverbs 11)

Southern Miss Finale

The LORD has done this, and it is marvelous in our eyes. The LORD has done it this very day; let us rejoice today and be glad. LORD, save us! LORD, grant us success! Blessed is he who comes in the name of the LORD. From the house of the LORD we bless you. The LORD is God, and he has made his light shine on us. With boughs in hand, join in the festal procession up to the horns of the altar. You are my God, and I will praise you; you are my God, and I will exalt you. Give thanks to the LORD, for he is good; his love endures forever. (Psalm 118:23-29)

Southern Miss vs UAB Highlights Video

"Southern Miss Finale" Narrative

C ontrol the things you can control. Coaches preach it. No coach has been forced to live it quite like UAB's Bill Clark during the final month of what appeared to be turning into the football program's final season.

After news broke in early November of 2014 that the school might actually drop the sport, Clark and his team searched for answers about the future but found none. In the face of that mounting uncertainty, they could've sagged, dragged or flat-out quit, especially after a heartbreaking loss to unbeaten Marshall in their final home game.

Instead, a week later, the Blazers arrived at Southern Miss for the last regular-season game with a fire in their eyes no opponent could extinguish.

With something to accomplish, something the players and coaches could control, the Blazers did it in dominant fashion, taking apart their rival 45-24. That victory evened their record at 6-6, the school's best in 10 years, and made them bowl-eligible for the first time in a decade.

They put aside the questions about their future to make a statement. If this were going to be the last game in school history, it would be remembered as an emphatic victory in the face of unthinkable adversity.

Documentary: "UAB Beats Southern Miss 45-24"

"Southern Miss Finale"

Chapter 12 Worship Song
Pentatonix "Hallelujah"

Have you, or someone you know, ever had something really great happen and then the bottom fall out soon thereafter?

Explain.

What applicable principle can you learn and apply from this observation?

Prayer: *Dear God I know that I must be careful when men praise me...Father,*

_____

_____

_____

Lesson 12 Coaching Point:

You must believe God steadfastly through both victory and defeat.

Steven Furtick Video Message
"God Is Bigger Than Your Battle"

Read Proverbs 12 (NIV) and highlight the phrases that speak to your heart:

Whoever loves discipline loves knowledge, but whoever hates correction is stupid. Good people obtain favor from the LORD, but he condemns those who devise wicked schemes. No one can be established through wickedness, but the righteous cannot be uprooted. A wife of noble character is her husband's crown, but a disgraceful wife is like decay in his bones. The plans of the righteous are just, but the advice of the wicked is deceitful. The words of the wicked lie in wait for blood, but the speech of the upright rescues them. The wicked are overthrown and are no more, but the house of the righteous stands firm. A person is praised according to their prudence, and one with a warped mind is despised. Better to be a nobody and yet have a servant than pretend to be somebody and have no food. The righteous care for the needs of their animals, but the kindest acts of the wicked are cruel. Those who work their land will have abundant food, but those who chase fantasies have no sense. The wicked desire the stronghold of evildoers, but the root of the righteous endures. Evildoers are trapped by their sinful talk, and so the innocent escape trouble. From the fruit of their lips people are filled with good things, and the work of their hands brings them reward. The way of fools seems right to them, but the wise listen to advice. Fools show their annoyance at once, but the prudent overlook an insult. An honest witness tells the truth, but a false witness tells lies. The words of the reckless pierce like swords, but the tongue of the wise brings healing. Truthful lips endure forever, but a lying tongue lasts only a moment. Deceit is in the hearts of those who plot evil, but those who promote peace have joy. No harm overtakes the righteous, but the wicked have their fill of trouble. The LORD *detests lying lips, but he delights in people who are trustworthy. The prudent keep their knowledge to themselves, but a fool's heart blurts out folly. Diligent hands will rule, but laziness ends in forced labor. Anxiety weighs down the heart, but a kind word cheers it up. The righteous choose their friends carefully, but the way of the wicked leads them astray. The lazy do not roast any game, but the diligent feed on the riches of the hunt. In the way of righteousness there is life; along that path is immortality.* (Proverbs 12)

Chapter 13

The Shutdown

My God, my God, why have you forsaken me? Why are you so far from saving me, so far from my cries of anguish? My God, I cry out by day, but you do not answer, by night, but I find no rest. Yet you are enthroned as the Holy One; you are the one Israel praises. In you our ancestors put their trust; they trusted and you delivered them. To you they cried out and were saved; in you they trusted and were not put to shame. (Psalm 22:1-5)

ESPN Shutdown Report (Video)

"The Shut Down" Narrative

I f the scene outside the old dentist office of a football building on the afternoon of December 2, 2014 didn't break your heart, you didn't have one.

It was the day UAB football died.

After hearing the news from University President Ray Watts in an emotional team meeting, players, coaches, and staffers emerged in a stunned procession of red eyes, raw hugs, and dashed hopes.

So many strong men shed so many honest tears.

Their blood, sweat, and tears didn't fit onto the university's balance sheet. Their hopes and dreams didn't figure into the outside consultant's strategic study. Their sport, their team, their family was going away, they were told, because the numbers didn't add up.

If you don't believe football is more than a game, you didn't see Dallas Noriega that day. The senior long snapper had made an indelible impression during rallies to try to save the program, waving the school flag, raising his fist and his voice. After hearing the death sentence, Noriega drifted to the pot-holed practice field. He was inconsolable, tears streaming down his face.

Somewhere in heaven that day, Gene Bartow must have been crying, too.

Documentary

"UAB Shutting Down Football Program"

"The Shut Down"

Chapter 13 Worship Song
Mercy Me-"Even If"

Do you, or someone you know, have a story of a time when God's Destiny seem to counteract what seemingly should have happened?

Explain.

What applicable principle can you learn and apply from this observation?

Prayer: *Dear God, You are sovereign and You have a plan. Just because I don't understand it doesn't mean something is wrong...Father,*

_____

_____

_____

Lesson 13 Coaching Point:
You must believe God is sovereign.

Joel Osteen Video Message
"It Is Finished"

Read Proverbs 13 (NIV) and highlight the phrases that speak to your heart:

A wise son heeds his father's instruction, but a mocker does not respond to rebukes. From the fruit of their lips people enjoy good things, but the unfaithful have an appetite for violence. Those who guard their lips preserve their lives, but those who speak rashly will come to ruin. A sluggard's appetite is never filled, but the desires of the diligent are fully satisfied. The righteous hate what is false, but the wicked make themselves a stench and bring shame on themselves. Righteousness guards the person of integrity, but wickedness overthrows the sinner. One person pretends to be rich, yet has nothing; another pretends to be poor, yet has great wealth. A person's riches may ransom their life, but the poor cannot respond to threatening rebukes. The light of the righteous shines brightly, but the lamp of the wicked is snuffed out. Where there is strife, there is pride, but wisdom is found in those who take advice. Dishonest money dwindles away, but whoever gathers money little by little makes it grow. Hope deferred makes the heart sick, but a longing fulfilled is a tree of life. Whoever scorns instruction will pay for it, but whoever respects a command is rewarded. The teaching of the wise is a fountain of life, turning a person from the snares of death. Good judgment wins favor, but the way of the unfaithful leads to their destruction. All who are prudent act with knowledge, but fools expose their folly. A wicked messenger falls into trouble, but a trustworthy envoy brings healing. Whoever disregards discipline comes to poverty and shame, but whoever heeds correction is honored. A longing fulfilled is sweet to the soul, but fools detest turning from evil. Walk with the wise and become wise, for a companion of fools suffers harm. Trouble pursues the sinner, but the righteous are rewarded with good things. A good person leaves an inheritance for their children's children, but a sinner's wealth is stored up for the righteous. An unplowed field produces food for the poor, but injustice sweeps it away. Whoever spares the rod hates their children, but the one who loves their children is careful to discipline them. The righteous eat to their hearts' content, but the stomach of the wicked goes hungry. (Proverbs 13)

Chapter 14

Scattered Abroad

A father to the fatherless, a defender of widows, is God
in his holy dwelling.
God sets the lonely in families, he leads out the prisoners
with singing; but the rebellious live in a sun-scorched
land. (Psalm 68:5-6)

The Final Meeting Scattered the Players Video

"Scattered Abroad" Narrative

T hey could break their hearts and take away their program. They could not take away their love of the game.

With the UAB football program shut down after the 2014 season, UAB's football players had a different kind of work to do. The vast majority still had college eligibility remaining, so they had to find new academic and athletic homes. The NCAA granted them immediate eligibility elsewhere, thanks to the unique nature of their reason for transferring and one after another, they took full advantage of the opportunity.

They became starting quarterbacks, standout receivers, and leading tacklers. They became immediate contributors on teams across the country, including programs in Power 5 Conferences such as the SEC, the ACC, and the Big Ten.

Jordan Howard, the workhorse running back, pounded the rock for Indiana and finished third in the Big Ten in rushing. Jake Ganus, the inside linebacker with a nose for the ball, led Georgia in tackles and was named the team's overall MVP and a permanent defensive captain.

They were just two of the many success stories of former Blazers who overcame circumstances beyond their control to prove themselves in their new homes. Look at that group as a whole and it's impossible not to wonder. How good would the 2015 UAB football team have been?

Documentary

"The 2014 UAB Blazers: Where Are They Now"

"Scattered Abroad"

Chapter 14 Worship Song
Lauren Daigle "Trust In You"

Have you, or someone that you know, seen a fatherless child or someone with little or no real blood family overcome those obstacles?

Explain.

What applicable principle can you learn and apply from this observation?

Prayer: *Dear God, You are always here for me no matter who else is not here for me...Father,*

_____

_____

_____

Lesson 14 Coaching Point:

You must believe God will take care of you even if no one else will.

Craig Groeschel Video Message
<u>"Dealing With Crippling Anxiety"</u>

Read Proverbs 14 (NIV) and highlight the phrases that speak to your heart:

The wise woman builds her house, but with her own hands the foolish one tears hers down. Whoever fears the LORD walks uprightly, but those who despise him are devious in their ways. A fool's mouth lashes out with pride, but the lips of the wise protect them. Where there are no oxen, the manger is empty, but from the strength of an ox come abundant harvests. An honest witness does not deceive, but a false witness pours out lies. The mocker seeks wisdom and finds none, but knowledge comes easily to the discerning. Stay away from a fool, for you will not find knowledge on their lips. The wisdom of the prudent is to give thought to their ways, but the folly of fools is deception. Fools mock at making amends for sin, but goodwill is found among the upright. Each heart knows its own bitterness, and no one else can share its joy. The house of the wicked will be destroyed, but the tent of the upright will flourish. There is a way that appears to be right, but in the end it leads to death. Even in laughter the heart may ache, and rejoicing may end in grief. The faithless will be fully repaid for their ways, and the good rewarded for theirs. The simple believe anything, but the prudent give thought to their steps. The wise fear the LORD and shun evil, but a fool is hotheaded and yet feels secure. A quick-tempered person does foolish things, and the one who devises evil schemes is hated. The simple inherit folly, but the prudent are crowned with knowledge. Evildoers will bow down in the presence of the good, and the wicked at the gates of the righteous. The poor are shunned even by their neighbors, but the rich have many friends. It is a sin to despise one's neighbor, but blessed is the one who is kind to the needy. Do not those who plot evil go astray? But those who plan what is good find love and faithfulness. All hard work brings a profit, but mere talk leads only to poverty. The wealth of the wise is their crown, but the folly of fools yields folly. A truthful witness saves lives, but a false witness is deceitful. Whoever fears the LORD has a secure fortress, and for their children it will be a refuge. The fear of the LORD is a fountain of life, turning a person from the snares of death. A large population is a king's glory, but without subjects a prince is ruined. Whoever is patient has great understanding, but one who is quick-tempered displays folly. A heart at peace gives life to the body, but envy rots the bones. Whoever oppresses the poor shows contempt for their Maker, but whoever is kind to the needy honors God. When calamity comes, the wicked are brought down, but even in death the righteous seek refuge in God. Wisdom reposes in the heart of the discerning and even among fools she lets herself be known. Righteousness exalts a nation, but sin condemns any people. A king delights in a wise servant, but a shameful servant arouses his fury. (Proverbs 14)

Chapter 15

How'd This Happen?

But if it is from God, you will not be able to stop these men; you will only find yourselves fighting against God."
(Acts 5:39)

Ty Long Interview Video

"How'd This Happen?" Narrative

U AB football may have ended on December 2, 2014, but the search for answers was only beginning. Local reporters obtained confidential documents and private recordings. The most fundamental question they pursued: Why?

Was it simply a lack of support, measured by booster donations and fan attendance, for a program that hadn't had a winning season since 2004? The tens of millions of dollars raised and the attendance records set since the program's reinstatement suggest not.

Or was it a lethal combination of UA System Board of Trustee indifference, interference, and disdain? That's the strong belief of UAB insiders, weary of being governed by a board with a large majority of members who graduated from the University of Alabama in Tuscaloosa and cheer first and foremost for the Crimson Tide.

Some of their evidence traces to the late Gene Bartow. In 1991, the father of UAB athletics had written a private letter urging the NCAA to investigate the Alabama basketball program. In that letter, made public by the LA Times in 1993, Bartow had made comments critical of the late Paul "Bear" Bryant, the legendary Alabama football coach.

Who was the most powerful UA System trustee at the time of the UAB football shutdown? Who was the board president who, three years earlier, had publicly voiced his opposition to UAB building an on-campus stadium? Paul Bryant Jr., the Bear's only son.

Bryant Jr. never spoke publicly about the decision to shut down the UAB football program. To many passionate UAB supporters, that decision spoke for itself - and for him.

Documentary
"Did Paul Bryant Jr. Really Kill UAB Football?"

Chapter 15 Worship Song

Danny Gokey "Tell Your Heart To Beat Again"

Can you, or someone you know, identify a time or an event where a group or team seemed destined from God to succeed and did in spite of authorities trying to stop them?

Explain.

What applicable principle can you learn and apply from this observation?

Prayer: *Dear God the devil can thwart me, but he has no authority over a born-again believer and if You put me on a mission I am destined to succeed...Father,*

_____

_____

_____

Lesson 15 Coaching Point:

You must believe God giving you a plan means that nothing can stop you.

Joel Osteen Video Message
<u>"Keep Strife Out of Your Life"</u>

Read Proverbs 15 (NIV) and highlight the phrases that speak to your heart:

A gentle answer turns away wrath, but a harsh word stirs up anger. The tongue of the wise adorns knowledge, but the mouth of the fool gushes folly. The eyes of the LORD are everywhere, keeping watch on the wicked and the good. The soothing tongue is a tree of life, but a perverse tongue crushes the spirit. A fool spurns a parent's discipline, but whoever heeds correction shows prudence. The house of the righteous contains great treasure, but the income of the wicked brings ruin. The lips of the wise spread knowledge, but the hearts of fools are not upright. The LORD detests the sacrifice of the wicked, but the prayer of the upright pleases him. The LORD detests the way of the wicked, but he loves those who pursue righteousness. Stern discipline awaits anyone who leaves the path; the one who hates correction will die. Death and Destruction lie open before the LORD-how much more do human hearts! Mockers resent correction, so they avoid the wise. A happy heart makes the face cheerful, but heartache crushes the spirit. The discerning heart seeks knowledge, but the mouth of a fool feeds on folly. All the days of the oppressed are wretched, but the cheerful heart has a continual feast. Better a little with the fear of the LORD than great wealth with turmoil. Better a small serving of vegetables with love than a fattened calf with hatred. A hot-tempered person stirs up conflict, but the one who is patient calms a quarrel. The way of the sluggard is blocked with thorns, but the path of the upright is a highway. A wise son brings joy to his father, but a foolish man despises his mother. Folly brings joy to one who has no sense, but whoever has understanding keeps a straight course. Plans fail for lack of counsel, but with many advisers they succeed. A person finds joy in giving an apt reply-and how good is a timely word! The path of life leads upward for the prudent to keep them from going down to the realm of the dead. The LORD tears down the house of the proud, but he sets the widow's boundary stones in place. The LORD detests the thoughts of the wicked, but gracious words are pure in his sight. The greedy bring ruin to their households, but the one who hates bribes will live. The heart of the righteous weighs its answers, but the mouth of the wicked gushes evil. The LORD is far from the wicked, but he hears the prayer of the righteous. Light in a messenger's eyes brings joy to the heart, and good news gives health to the bones. Whoever heeds life-giving correction will be at home among the wise.

Those who disregard discipline despise themselves, but the one who heeds correction gains understanding. Wisdom's instruction is to fear the LORD, and humility comes before honor. (Proverbs 15)

Chapter 16

#The Return

The angel said to the women, "Do not be afraid, for I know that you are looking for Jesus, who was crucified. He is not here; he has risen, just as he said. Come and see the place where he lay." (Matthew 28:5-6)

Ray Watts Reinstatement Speech Video

"#The Return" Narrative

A funny thing happened after the death of UAB football. The program found new life. It was as if a sleeping dragon had been awakened, and he rose up, breathing fire.

A passionate army of students, faculty, alumni, former players, boosters, and fans in the streets of Birmingham and beyond, outraged at a shutdown they believed fundamentally unfair, rallied to bring back the program. Their most important mission was raising the $17 million the administration said was needed to restore the program.

The money came from near and far, in amounts great and small. A 5-year-old from Dublin, Ohio, who simply liked UAB's Blaze the Dragon mascot and logo, mailed in his $1 allowance to contribute to the cause. A group of Birmingham business leaders, who understood UAB's prominent place in the community, took the fundraising lead and became an unstoppable force.

At the most memorable meeting of that group, which came to be known as the Gang of Seven, Mike Goodrich Sr. inspired the room with this declaration: "I'm not a UAB fan. I don't think I've ever been to a game. But I've seen what this has done to our community, and I want to make it right. I'm in for a million."

Others followed suit with major gifts, and before that meeting ended, the fundraising campaign had met its goal. The UAB administrators in the room had seen the light. UAB football would return to the field in two years and two months, but with no players and substandard facilities, there was still a long, hard road ahead.

Documentary

"UAB Reinstates Football for 2016"

"#The Return"

Chapter 16 Worship Song
Elevation Worship "Resurrecting"

Have you, or someone you know, ever witnessed somebody be born again?

Explain.

What applicable principle can you learn and apply from this observation?

Prayer: *Dear God I know that something has to die in order to see a resurrection...Father,*

_____

_____

_____

Lesson 16 Coaching Point:

You must believe God gave you the resurrection power of Jesus.

Craig Groeschel Video Message
"I'm Over It"

Read Proverbs 16 (NIV) and highlight the phrases that speak to your heart:

To humans belong the plans of the heart, but from the LORD comes the proper answer of the tongue. All a person's ways seem pure to them, but motives are weighed by the LORD. Commit to the LORD whatever you do, and he will establish your plans. The LORD works out everything to its proper end-even the wicked for a day of disaster. The LORD detests all the proud of heart. Be sure of this: They will not go unpunished. Through love and faithfulness sin is atoned for; through the fear of the LORD evil is avoided. When the LORD takes pleasure in anyone's way, he causes their enemies to make peace with them.

Better a little with righteousness than much gain with injustice. In their hearts humans plan their course, but the LORD establishes their steps. The lips of a king speak as an oracle, and his mouth does not betray justice. Honest scales and balances belong to the LORD; all the weights in the bag are of his making. Kings detest wrongdoing, for a throne is established through righteousness. Kings take pleasure in honest lips; they value the one who speaks what is right. A king's wrath is a messenger of death, but the wise will appease it. When a king's face brightens, it means life; his favor is like a rain cloud in spring. How much better to get wisdom than gold, to get insight rather than silver! The highway of the upright avoids evil; those who guard their ways preserve their lives. Pride goes before destruction, a haughty spirit before a fall. Better to be lowly in spirit along with the oppressed than to share plunder with the proud. Whoever gives heed to instruction prospers, and blessed is the one who trusts in the LORD. The wise in heart are called discerning, and gracious words promote instruction. Prudence is a fountain of life to the prudent, but folly brings punishment to fools. The hearts of the wise make their mouths prudent, and their lips promote instruction. Gracious words are a honeycomb, sweet to the soul and healing to the bones. There is a way that appears to be right, but in the end it leads to death. The appetite of laborers works for them; their hunger drives them on. A scoundrel plots evil, and on their lips it is like a scorching fire. A perverse person stirs up conflict, and a gossip separates close friends. A violent person entices their neighbor and leads them down a path that is not good. Whoever winks with their eye is plotting perversity; whoever purses their lips is bent on evil. Gray hair is a crown of splendor; it is attained in the way of righteousness. Better a patient person than a warrior, one with self-control than one who takes a city. The lot is cast into the lap, but its every decision is from the LORD. (Proverbs 16)

Chapter 17

The Staff, The Originals, and Hope for the Future

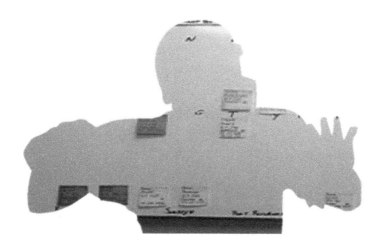

"Come, follow me," Jesus said, "and I will send you out to fish for people." (Matthew 4:19)

We're Back (Video)

"The Staff, The Originals, and Hope for the Future" Narrative

"Coach Pippin, it'll change but for right now I'm going to make you the Director of Player Personnel," Coach Clark said. "The good news is we officially have a FBS football team here at UAB. The bad news is we only have 16 players as represented by these color-coded sticky notes on the board. Also, we will be expected to compete in C-USA in 2 years. Start recruiting, and by the way, there is a young man at Shannon's desk that wants to talk to someone about coming out for the team."

"Yes sir, I'll meet him now."

"Hello there, young man, you have the dubious distinction of being the first young man to seek a roster spot, what is your name?"

"Jesus," said the nice-looking young man.

"Excuse me?" I replied.

"Yes, sir, Jesus Perez," he said.

"Okay, fill this out and give it to Shannon then we will be having a tryout in 2 weeks so check back for exacts," I said. "We are having our day end staff meeting now that I need to get to."

"Hey Coach Walker, we have just had our first guy inquire about walking on and his name is Jesus."

Coach Walker without hesitation then responded with, "Then we need to accept him."

We then met to find out what the rules of engagement were going to be here with UAB director of compliance Cory Bray. We were informed that we have a year to freeze the clock and not count against a kid's eligibility. Also, during that year, if we can get them in school with a 2.0 GPA or better since we are not playing, we can get them eligible if they make satisfactory progress and be honorable citizens as well.

"Good luck," said Cory Bray.

So, we were off to the races setting up camps, clinics, high school visits, JUCO visits, College/NFL practice visits, and trying to find the rest of the best players available in one of the 140 Junior Colleges coast to coast.

"Let's reel them in men!"

Documentary
"Meet The 2016 UAB Football Coaches"

"The Staff, The Originals, and Hope for the Future"

Chapter 17 Worship Song
Hillsong United "No Other Name – Oceans"

Have you, or someone you know, ever fished for people? Explain.

What applicable principle can you learn and apply from this observation?

Prayer: *Dear God one of Your greatest commissions is to recruit people for Your kingdom work...Father,*

_____

_____

_____

Lesson 17 Coaching Point:
You must believe God has called you to fish for people.

Joel Osteen Video Message
"Take Your Seat"

Read Proverbs 17 (NIV) and highlight the phrases that speak to your heart:

Better a dry crust with peace and quiet than a house full of feasting, with strife. A prudent servant will rule over a disgraceful son and will share the inheritance as one of the family. The crucible for silver and the furnace for gold, but the LORD tests the heart. A wicked person listens to deceitful lips; a liar pays attention to a destructive tongue. Whoever mocks the poor shows contempt for their Maker; whoever gloats over disaster will not go unpunished. Children's children are a crown to the aged, and parents are the pride of their children. Eloquent lips are unsuited to a godless fool-how much worse lying lips to a ruler! A bribe is seen as a charm by the one who gives it; they think success will come at every turn. Whoever would foster love covers over an offense, but whoever repeats the matter separates close friends. A rebuke impresses a discerning person more than a hundred lashes a fool. Evildoers foster rebellion against God; the messenger of death will be sent against them. Better to meet a bear robbed of her cubs than a fool bent on folly. Evil will never leave the house of one who pays back evil for good. Starting a quarrel is like breaching a dam; so drop the matter before a dispute breaks out. Acquitting the guilty and condemning the innocent-the LORD *detests them both. Why should fools have money in hand to buy wisdom, when they are not able to understand it? A friend loves at all times, and a brother is born for a time of adversity. One who has no sense shakes hands in pledge and puts up security for a neighbor. Whoever loves a quarrel loves sin; whoever builds a high gate invites destruction. One whose heart is corrupt does not prosper; one whose tongue is perverse falls into trouble. To have a fool for a child brings grief; there is no joy for the parent of a godless fool. A cheerful heart is good medicine, but a crushed spirit dries up the bones. The wicked accept bribes in secret to pervert the course of justice. A discerning person keeps wisdom in view, but a fool's eyes wander to the ends of the earth. A foolish son brings grief to his father and bitterness to the mother who bore him. If imposing a fine on the innocent is not good, surely to flog honest officials is not right. The one who has knowledge uses words with restraint, and whoever has understanding is even-tempered. Even fools are thought wise if they keep silent, and discerning if they hold their tongues.* (Proverbs 17)

Chapter 18

Resurrecting Opportunities

And if the Spirit of him who raised Jesus from the dead is living in you, he who raised Christ from the dead will also give life to your mortal bodies because of[a] his Spirit who lives in you. Therefore, brothers and sisters, we have an obligation-but it is not to the flesh, to live according to it. For if you live according to the flesh, you will die; but if by the Spirit you put to death the misdeeds of the body, you will live. (Romans 8:11-13)

First Spring Practice Story Video

"Resurrecting Opportunities" Narrative

Bill Clark didn't stay in Birmingham to lose. He didn't endure the uncertain months between The Shutdown and The Return of UAB football to put together a team full of high school recruits who weren't big enough, strong enough, and experienced enough to compete in Conference USA when the program returned to the field in 2017.

Two years wasn't enough time to start completely from scratch. The head coach wanted older players, players as hungry as the fan base, players who may have faced adversity, and would appreciate the opportunity the Blazers could provide. UAB had been given a second chance as a football program. Clark was determined to provide that same kind of second chance to players who needed someone to believe in them again.

So, he welcomed junior college players and transfers from four-year schools, some of them former big-name recruits who hadn't lived up to that billing for one reason or another. Clark wasn't offering them a chance to make the same mistake twice. He was presenting them an opportunity to demonstrate that they'd learned from their mistakes in a loving, caring, disciplined environment.

Every one of those early recruits had a distinct story that led them to Birmingham, where so many of them would try to make a comeback with the ultimate comeback program.

Documentary

"UAB: The Dead Program That's Stockpiling Blue-Chip Recruits"

"Resurrecting Opportunities"

Chapter 18 Worship Song
Mercy Me - Flawless

Have you, or someone you know, ever made a commitment to give up a practice or habit in your life that you knew was wrong or harmful and found yourself feeling better?

Explain.

What applicable principle can you learn and apply from this observation?

Prayer: *Dear God I know that there is pain in discipline and I also know that there is much more pain in regret...Father,*

_____

_____

_____

Lesson 18 Coaching Point:

You must believe God requires either the pain of discipline or the pain of regret.

Steven Furtick Video Message
"Opportunity Is Knocking"

Read Proverbs 18 (NIV) and highlight the phrases that speak to your heart:

An unfriendly person pursues selfish ends and against all sound judgment starts quarrels. Fools find no pleasure in understanding but delight in airing their own opinions. When wickedness comes, so does contempt, and with shame comes reproach. The words of the mouth are deep waters, but the fountain of wisdom is a rushing stream. It is not good to be partial to the wicked and so deprive the innocent of justice. The lips of fools bring them strife, and their mouths invite a beating. The mouths of fools are their undoing, and their lips are a snare to their very lives. The words of a gossip are like choice morsels; they go down to the inmost parts. One who is slack in his work is brother to one who destroys. The name of the LORD is a fortified tower; the righteous run to it and are safe. The wealth of the rich is their fortified city; they imagine it a wall too high to scale. Before a downfall the heart is haughty, but humility comes before honor. To answer before listening-that is folly and shame. The human spirit can endure in sickness, but a crushed spirit who can bear? The heart of the discerning acquires knowledge, for the ears of the wise seek it out. A gift opens the way and ushers the giver into the presence of the great. In a lawsuit the first to speak seems right, until someone comes forward and cross-examines. Casting the lot settles disputes and keeps strong opponents apart. A brother wronged is more unyielding than a fortified city; disputes are like the barred gates of a citadel. From the fruit of their mouth a person's stomach is filled; with the harvest of their lips they are satisfied. The tongue has the power of life and death, and those who love it will eat its fruit. He who finds a wife finds what is good and receives favor from the LORD. *The poor plead for mercy, but the rich answer harshly. One who has unreliable friends soon comes to ruin, but there is a friend who sticks closer than a brother.* (Proverbs 18)

Chapter 19

Greg Bryant Murdered

For God so loved the world that he gave His one and only Son, that whoever believes in Him shall not perish but have eternal life. (John 3:16)

Death By Greg Bryant Video

"Greg Bryant Murdered" Narrative

Of all the players UAB took a chance on, of all the players who took a chance on UAB, none brought a bigger name to Birmingham than Greg Bryant.

The Florida product had been one of the top high school running backs in the nation. He'd signed with an elite college program in Notre Dame. After two underwhelming years with the Fighting Irish, on the eve of what everyone hoped would be a breakout junior season, he was declared academically ineligible.

At the point where too many promising careers end, determined not to give up on himself, Bryant left South Bend for a south Florida junior college. His hard road back led him to the perfect place for a player in search of redemption: UAB.

Bryant found a new home in Birmingham, impressing his teammates and coaches with his effort on the field and in the classroom. Then he went home to see his mom for Mother's Day 2016. He would not return.

Bryant was murdered in a drive-by shooting on the interstate in West Palm Beach. The timing and suddenness of the cold-blooded killing was beyond comprehension. How would the fragile, upstart Blazers handle such a terrible tragedy?

Documentary: <u>On the legacy of UAB's Greg Bryant, the second-chance star of the second-chance team</u>

"Greg Bryant Murdered"

Chapter 19 Worship Song
Newsong "ARISE MY LOVE"

Have you, or someone you know, lost someone in your life to death but known that they were in heaven because of their acknowledgment of Jesus as Lord?

Explain.

What applicable principle can you learn and apply from this observation?

Prayer: *Dear God, when I die it is final and only one thing matters, did I accept Jesus Christ as my Lord and Savior while I was living...Father,*

_____

_____

_____

Lesson 19 Coaching Point:

You must believe God sent His Son so you could have eternal life.

Craig Groeschel Video Message
"The Faith to Forgive-The Grudge"

Read Proverbs 19 (NIV) and highlight the phrases that speak to your heart:

Better the poor whose walk is blameless than a fool whose lips are perverse. Desire without knowledge is not good-how much more will hasty feet miss the way! A person's own folly leads to their ruin, yet their heart rages against the LORD. Wealth attracts many friends but even the closest friend of the poor person deserts them. A false witness will not go unpunished, and whoever pours out lies will not go free. Many curry favor with a ruler, and everyone is the friend of one who gives gifts. The poor are shunned by all their relatives-how much more do their friends avoid them! Though the poor pursue them with pleading, they are nowhere to be found. The one who gets wisdom loves life; the one who cherishes understanding will soon prosper. A false witness will not go unpunished, and whoever pours out lies will perish. It is not fitting for a fool to live in luxury-how much worse for a slave to rule over princes! A person's wisdom yields patience; it is to one's glory to overlook an offense. A king's rage is like the roar of a lion, but his favor is like dew on the grass.

A foolish child is a father's ruin, and a quarrelsome wife is like the constant dripping of a leaky roof. Houses and wealth are inherited from parents, but a prudent wife is from the Lord. Laziness brings on deep sleep, and the shiftless go hungry. Whoever keeps commandments keeps their life, but whoever shows contempt for their ways will die. Whoever is kind to the poor lends to the Lord, and he will reward them for what they have done. Discipline your children, for in that there is hope; do not be a willing party to their death. A hot-tempered person must pay the penalty; rescue them, and you will have to do it again. Listen to advice and accept discipline, and at the end you will be counted among the wise. Many are the plans in a person's heart, but it is the Lord's purpose that prevails. What a person desires is unfailing love; better to be poor than a liar. The fear of the Lord leads to life; then one rests content, untouched by trouble. A sluggard buries his hand in the dish; he will not even bring it back to his mouth! (Proverb 19)

Rising from the Ashes in Preparation

Raise a banner on a bare hilltop, shout to them; beckon to them to enter the gates of the nobles. I have commanded those I prepared for battle; I have summoned my warriors to carry out my wrath-those who rejoice in my triumph. Listen, a noise on the mountains, like that of a great multitude! Listen, an uproar among the kingdoms, like nations massing together! The LORD Almighty is mustering an army for war. (Isaiah 13:2-4)

Green and Gold Game (Video)

"Rising From the Ashes in Preparation" Narrative

With Greg Bryant buried and his spirit living on in the locker room and in the hearts of the team, the Blazers continued to rise out of the southern urban landscape.

The summer and fall of 2016 was treated much like a regular season without an opponent to look forward to competing against. The opponent was one's own UAB teammates that could keep you from earning your spot on the roster. The other opponent was whatever intensity levels the coaches could create for you to best simulate what you would be facing.

One Coach proved to be a master at creating an environment that could best simulate the intensity and ruthless, relentless ferocity of facing another FBS college opponent.

"Up downs! Now!" became known as one coach's mantra and his hard coaching planted seeds to help make game day a little easier.

Football is hard, and so is life. Football many times seems unfair and so does life. Football teaches you that you will get knocked down and so does life. Football teaches you that in order to succeed you must get back up and shake it off and so does life.

Documentary
"UAB Blazers Rise from Ashes, Eager to Resume Playing Football"

"Rising from The Ashes in Preparation"

Chapter 20 Worship Song
Jeremy Camp "Overcome"

Have you, or someone you know, ever watched an organization emerge and become powerful because of dedicated people? Explain.

What applicable principle can you learn and apply from this observation?

Prayer: *Dear God when You pull a group of men together, that group will be a powerful entity...Father,*

_____

_____

_____

Lesson 20 Coaching Point:
You must believe God summons people to be warriors.

Steve Furtick Video Message
"Don't Let The Enemy Distract You"

Read Proverbs 20 (NIV) and highlight the phrases that speak to your heart:

Wine is a mocker and beer a brawler; whoever is led astray by them is not wise. A king's wrath strikes terror like the roar of a lion; those who anger him forfeit their lives. It is to one's honor to avoid strife, but every fool is quick to quarrel. Sluggards do not plow in season; so at harvest time they look but find nothing. The purposes of a person's heart are deep waters, but one who has insight draws them out. Many claim to have unfailing love, but a faithful person who can find? The righteous lead blameless lives; blessed are their children after them. When a king sits on his throne to judge, he winnows out all evil with his eyes. Who can say, "I have kept my heart pure; I am clean and without sin"? Differing weights and differing measures-the LORD detests them both. Even small children are known by their actions, so is their conduct really pure and upright? Ears that hear and eyes that see-the LORD has made them both. Do not love sleep or you will grow poor; stay awake and you will have food to spare. "It's no good, it's no good!" says the buyer-then goes off and boasts about the purchase. Gold there is, and rubies in abundance, but lips that speak knowledge are a rare jewel. Take the garment of one who puts up security for a stranger; hold it in pledge if it is done for an outsider. Food gained by fraud tastes sweet, but one ends up with a mouth full of gravel. Plans are established by seeking advice; so if you wage war, obtain guidance. A gossip betrays a confidence; so avoid anyone who talks too much. If someone curses their father or mother, their lamp will be snuffed out in pitch darkness. An inheritance claimed too soon will not be blessed at the end. Do not say, "I'll pay you back for this wrong!" Wait for the LORD, *and he will avenge you. The* LORD *detests differing weights, and dishonest scales do not please him. A person's steps are directed by the* LORD. *How then can anyone understand their own way? It is a trap to dedicate something rashly and only later to consider one's vows. A wise king winnows out the wicked; he drives the threshing wheel over them. The human spirit is the lamp of the* LORD *that sheds light on one's inmost being. Love and faithfulness keep a king safe; through love his throne is made secure. The glory of young men is their strength, gray hair the splendor of the old. Blows and wounds scrub away evil, and beatings purge the inmost being.* (Proverbs 20)

Chapter 21

Recruiting the Dudes

Then he said to me, "Prophesy to the breath; prophesy, son of man, and say to it, 'This is what the Sovereign LORD says: Come, breath, from the four winds and breathe into these slain, that they may live.'" So I prophesied as he commanded me, and breath entered them; they came to life and stood up on their feet-a vast army. (Ezekiel 37:9-10)

2016 Mid-Year Signees Recap Video

"Recruiting the Dudes" Narrative

C oach Clark's group of hand selected coaches and support staff continued on a relentless journey from coast to coast to find the best junior college and major college transfers they could get their hands on in order to have some guys with some age to start with and then follow it with a high school group. There was no blueprint because this had never been done before. The only really somewhat similar cases were the tragic Marshall University football team plane crash and the SMU "death penalty" for program violations. Both of these situations left virtually no players and thus required a comeback from scratch. For the most part, both of those schools used a more conventional recruiting style with mostly high school athletes. The result in both cases were many years of many losing seasons. UAB couldn't afford too many years of losing seasons.

The NCAA had made a few provisions in a short window to get in some guys that may not have been obtainable otherwise. So, freaks began to appear on campus and one of the best recruiting classes in the nation was put together in spite of the Blazers not playing until 2017.

Along with the volumes of new players coming, came volumes of stories. Once a receiver from Maryland via Iowa was caught stealing a significant amount of the new Under Armour gear. Upon being questioned by his position coach about taking the stuff he replied to him, "Bro I am from Baltimore and you have no idea of how much Under Armour stuff I have."

In another instance on a recruiting trip to California as one of the coaches battled the bay area traffic in an effort to get to San Francisco a 400 pound chain gang member slipped by the car on his motorcycle and slapped the rear view mirror breaking it off of the door and shot him the middle finger then proceeded weaving through the traffic never to be seen again.

In one of my favorite stories regarding coaching players on their body composition, a coach looked at his running backs 22 percent body fat documentation and told him that he was going to need to bring that down some. The player confidently replied, "Coach, you don't understand, I play good with extra body fat."

So, for more than 2 years, the UAB football family lived in this world of recruiting, character education, nutrition understanding, physical training, mindset development, academic support, and hopeful anticipation for the kickoff in 2017.

Documentary

"Clark Announces 2016 Recruiting Class"

"Recruiting the Dudes"

Chapter 21 Worship Song
I Surrender - Hillsong Worship

Have you, or someone you know, ever witnessed a person or group of people that were peculiar or freakish in nature but extremely talented at something?

Explain.

What applicable principle can you learn and apply from this observation?

Prayer: *Dear God, when You bring something back to life it seems more amazing than anything else anyone could orchestrate...Father,*

_____

_____

_____

Lesson 21 Coaching Point:
You must believe God will bring His people back to life.

Joel Osteen Video Message
"More Than Enough"

Read Proverbs 21 (NIV) and highlight the phrases that speak to your heart:

In the LORD's hand the king's heart is a stream of water that he channels toward all who please him. A person may think their own ways are right, but the LORD weighs the heart. To do what is right and just is more acceptable to the LORD than sacrifice. Haughty eyes and a proud heart-the unplowed field of the wicked-produce sin. The plans of the diligent lead to profit as surely as haste leads to poverty. A fortune made by a lying tongue is a fleeting vapor and a deadly snare. The violence of the wicked will drag them away, for they refuse to do what is right. The way of the guilty is devious, but the conduct of the innocent is upright. Better to live on a corner of the roof than share a house with a quarrelsome wife. The wicked crave evil; their neighbors get no mercy from them. When a mocker is punished, the simple gain wisdom; by paying attention to the wise they get knowledge. The Righteous One takes note of the house of the wicked and brings the wicked to ruin. Whoever shuts their ears to the cry of the poor will also cry out and not be answered. A gift given in secret soothes anger, and a bribe concealed in the cloak pacifies great wrath. When justice is done, it brings joy to the righteous but terror to evildoers. Whoever strays from the path of prudence comes to rest in the company of the dead. Whoever loves pleasure will become poor; whoever loves wine and olive oil will never be rich. The wicked become a ransom for the righteous, and the unfaithful for the upright. Better to live in a desert than with a quarrelsome and nagging wife. The wise store up choice food and olive oil, but fools gulp theirs down. Whoever pursues righteousness and love finds life, prosperity and honor. One who is wise can go up against the city of the mighty and pull down the stronghold in which they trust. Those who guard their mouths and their tongues keep themselves from calamity. The proud and arrogant person-"Mocker" is his name-behaves with insolent fury. The craving of a sluggard will be the death of him, because his hands refuse to work. All day long he craves for more, but the righteous give without sparing. The sacrifice of the wicked is detestable-how much more so when brought with evil intent! A false witness will perish, but a careful listener will testify successfully. The wicked put up a bold front, but the upright give thought to their ways. There is no wisdom, no insight, no plan that can succeed against the Lord. *The horse is made ready for the day of battle, but victory rests with the* Lord. (Proverbs 21)

Chapter 22

Retaining the Dogs

But the LORD said to Gideon, "There are still too many men. Take them down to the water, and I will thin them out for you there. If I say, 'This one shall go with you,' he shall go; but if I say, 'This one shall not go with you,' he shall not go." So Gideon took the men down to the water. There the LORD told him, "Separate those who lap the water with their tongues as a dog laps from those who kneel down to drink." Three hundred of them drank from cupped hands, lapping like dogs. All the rest got down on their knees to drink. The LORD said to Gideon, "With the three hundred men that lapped I will save you and give the Midianites into your hands. Let all the others go home." (Judges 7:4-6)

NLI Signing Day 2017 Recap Video

"Retaining the Dogs" Narrative

The most intriguing piece of this book and the essence of the heart are the stories of the players and who they are, where they come from, and what they've been through.

In no particular order, here are a few thumbnail sketches of #The Return Blazers that graduated. This is an effort to give a little taste from a very small percentage of stories upon stories originating from deep in the heart.

WR Sederian Copeland, Dallas: Unbelievable stats and talent, but slim and overlooked top duel threat JUCO QB.

WR Andre Wilson, San Antonio: Poster child for dynamic skilled athlete that overcame a bad English grade to be the best Blazer receiver.

FS Broderick Thomas, Houston: Big hitter, but bounced around until UAB gave him a shot then he made the biggest hit ever vs UTSA.

DT Garrett Marino, Southern California: Punched a bad kid with a bad attitude and got dismissed from JUCO eventually becoming an NFL prospect.

WR Xavier Ubosi, Los Angeles: Phenomenal size and speed, but immature and lost in Los Angeles JUCO but found in Birmingham.

WR Ronnie Turner Jr., Northern California: Phenomenal stats with his QB brother, but had to be with him so they both came to UAB.

OC Lee Dufour, Saraland: Went to South Alabama upon shutdown but came back to be Remington Award candidate.

QB AJ Erdely, Atlanta: Victim of circumstance at MTSU, went JUCO, came to UAB and settled up with MTSU.

RB James Noble III, Barstow: Walk-on that was the "poster child" for great team player and ended up with biggest picture in the building.

DE Shaq Jones, Lanette: Tall Safety in HS that became an E/OLB and was one of the originals from 2014.

PK Nick Vogel, Jacksonville: Went to Southern Miss upon the shutdown but came back and ended up in the Hula Bowl.

LB Tevin Crews, Tuscaloosa: Another versatile LB that was one of the originals from 2014.

NG Anthony Rush, Raleigh: Bounced around places through HS until JUCO coach finished raising him. Eventually became an NFL player.

WR Collin Lisa, North Georgia: Came back from the University of Buffalo to UAB and was Mr. Clutch.

OT James Davis, South Mississippi: One of the stars of Last Chance U and started virtually every game on OL.

SS Durez Diggs, Baltimore: NFL bloodline of brothers but made a name for himself.

RB DJ Law, Tampa: Last Chance U star everyone loved.

DT Teko Powell, Miami: Broke foot at Illinois, but came and impacted UAB until the Bahamas Bowl.

WR Kailon Carter, New Orleans: Bounced all over the country and paid way to UAB to become a star.

OG Chris Schluger, Iowa City: Went from FCS school to JUCO chasing the FBS dream and it worked.

LB Chris Woolbright New York City: From the Bronx NY to California JUCO to UAB Champion.

DE Kylin Binn, South Carolina: South Carolina State to Kansas JUCO as a QB and played it all at UAB.

DE Stacey Keely, Omaha: A twin in a 6-7 version that blocked a FG heard round the world. Eventually landed with the Minnesota Vikings.

LB Craig Kanyangarara, Lynn Massachusetts: AKA C4 from Zimbabwe to Massachusetts to Arizona JUCO to Birmingham and as hard of a worker as is on the planet.

DT Quindarius Thagard, Luverne: Big, strong and dependable as they come. Destined to be a law enforcement agent if not a pro football player.

OG Malique Johnson, Chicago: From Illinois to Iowa to UAB. A road grater for RBs.

DB Darious Williams, Jacksonville: From a walk-on to a flower delivery guy to the Super Bowl 2019 for the LA Rams.

ATH Donnie Lee, New Orleans: An accomplished 2 sport star before UAB coming from Arkansas Baptist as a Corner eventually playing Safety, Linebacker, Running Back, H-Back and Tight End. Real deal.

*There are too many others to mention and we are barely only scratching the surface.

Documentary

<u>"2017 Roster"</u>

"Retaining the Dogs"

Chapter 22 Worship Song

Tasha Cobbs – "Break Every Chain"

Have you, or someone you know, ever seen a large group culled to a smaller more elite group?

Explain.

What applicable principle can you learn and apply from this observation?

Prayer: *Dear God I know that a chain is only as strong as its weakest link...Father,*

_____

_____

_____

Lesson 22 Coaching Point:

You must believe God calls certain people to be on certain teams.

Steven Furtick Video Message
<u>"You Can't Win In Isolation"</u>

Read Proverbs 22 (NIV) and highlight the phrases that speak to your heart:

A good name is more desirable than great riches; to be esteemed is better than silver or gold. Rich and poor have this in common: The LORD is the Maker of them all. The prudent see danger and take refuge, but the simple keep going and pay the penalty. Humility is the fear of the LORD; its wages are riches and honor and life. In the paths of the wicked are snares and pitfalls, but those who would preserve their life stay far from them. Start children off on the way they should go, and even when they are old they will not turn from it. The rich rule over the poor, and the borrower is slave to the lender. Whoever sows injustice reaps calamity, and the rod they wield in fury will be broken. The generous will themselves be blessed, for they share their food with the poor. Drive out the mocker, and out goes strife; quarrels and insults are ended. One who loves a pure heart and who speaks with grace will have the king for a friend. The eyes of the LORD keep watch over knowledge, but he frustrates the words of the unfaithful. The sluggard says, "There's a lion outside! I'll be killed in the public square!" The mouth of an adulterous woman is a deep pit; a man who is under the LORD's wrath falls into it. Folly is bound up in the heart of a child, but the rod of discipline will drive it far away. One who oppresses the poor to increase his wealth and one who gives gifts to the rich-both come to poverty. (Proverbs 22)

Thirty Sayings of the Wise Beginning with Proverbs 22:17-29

Saying 1: (verses 17-21)

Pay attention and turn your ear to the sayings of the wise; apply your heart to what I teach, for it is pleasing when you keep them in your heart and have all of them ready on your lips. So that your trust may be in the LORD, I teach you today, even you. Have I not written thirty sayings for you, sayings of counsel and knowledge, teaching you to be honest and to speak the truth, so that you bring back truthful reports to those you serve?

Saying 2: (verses 22-23)

Do not exploit the poor because they are poor and do not crush the needy in court, for the LORD will take up their case and will exact life for life.

Saying 3: (verses 24-25)

Do not make friends with a hot-tempered person, do not associate with one easily angered, or you may learn their ways and get yourself ensnared.

Saying 4: (verses 26-27)

Do not be one who shakes hands in pledge or puts up security for debts; if you lack the means to pay, your very bed will be snatched from under you.

Saying 5: (verse 28)

Do not move an ancient boundary stone set up by your ancestors.

Saying 6: (verse 29)

Do you see someone skilled in their work? They will serve before kings; they will not serve before officials of low rank.

Chapter 23

New House

By wisdom a house is built, and through understanding it is established. (Proverbs 24:3)

Football Team Tours New Facility Video

"New House" Narrative

A groundbreaking. That's what they call it when they first put ceremonial shovels in the dirt to begin construction on a new building.

UAB brought new meaning to the word on August 29, 2016. Less than 15 months after the announcement that football would return, the head coach, athletics director, university president, and other dignitaries plunged gold shovels into the soil on one of the rocky old practice fields. They marked the spot that would contain the first capital project in the program's history: the $22.5-million, 46,000-square-foot Football Operations Center and Legacy Pavilion.

UAB had never made that kind of investment in football before.

A year later, just in time for fall camp, the Blazers moved into their new home, a state-of-the-art complex that included meeting rooms, locker room, training room, weight room, and coaches' offices, overlooking two new turf practice fields, one of them protected from the elements by a towering pavilion visible to everyone passing by on Interstate-65.

It was more than a big building. It was a major statement of the commitment made by so many UAB supporters who raised the money to pay for it. They had vowed not just to bring the program back but to give it a real chance to compete.

From start to finish, it was groundbreaking and breathtaking, and on the eve of #TheReturn, it was mission accomplished.

Documentary

<u>"UAB Blazers finally get to prepare for a game again"</u>

"New House"

Chapter 23 Worship Song
Newsboys – "We Believe"

What was and how did you get to the best place that you, or someone you know, ever lived?

Explain.

What applicable principle can you learn and apply from this observation?

Prayer: *Dear God Where we live is where we develop and therefore extremely important...Father,*

_____

_____

_____

Lesson 23 Coaching Point:

You must believe God wants you to have a good house.

Craig Groeschel Video Message
<u>"Do The Work. Make A Difference."</u>

Read Proverbs 23 (NIV) and highlight the phrases that speak to your heart:

Wise Sayings #7-19

Proverbs 23

Saying 7: (verses 1-3)

When you sit to dine with a ruler, note well what is before you, and put a knife to your throat if you are given to gluttony. Do not crave his delicacies, for that food is deceptive.

Saying 8: (verses 4-5)

Do not wear yourself out to get rich; do not trust your own cleverness. Cast but a glance at riches, and they are gone, for they will surely sprout wings and fly off to the sky like an eagle.

Saying 9: (verses 6-8)

Do not eat the food of a begrudging host, do not crave his delicacies; for he is the kind of person who is always thinking about the cost. "Eat and drink," he says to you, but his heart is not with you. You will vomit up the little you have eaten and will have wasted your compliments.

Saying 10: (verse 9)

Do not speak to fools for they will scorn your prudent words.

Saying 11: (verses 10-11)

Do not move an ancient boundary stone or encroach on the fields of the fatherless, for their Defender is strong; he will take up their case against you.

Saying 12: (verse 12)

Apply your heart to instruction and your ears to words of knowledge.

Saying 13: (verses 13-14)

Do not withhold discipline from a child; if you punish them with the rod, they will not die. Punish them with the rod and save them from death.

Saying 14: (verses 15-16)

My son, if your heart is wise, then my heart will be glad indeed; my inmost being will rejoice when your lips speak what is right.

Saying 15: (verses 17-18)

Do not let your heart envy sinners, but always be zealous for the fear of the LORD. There is surely a future hope for you, and your hope will not be cut off.

Saying 16: (verses 19-21)

Listen, my son, and be wise, and set your heart on the right path: Do not join those who drink too much wine or gorge themselves on meat, for drunkards and gluttons become poor, and drowsiness clothes them in rags.

Saying 17: (verses 22-25)

Listen to your father, who gave you life, and do not despise your mother when she is old. Buy the truth and do not sell it-wisdom, instruction and insight as well. The father of a righteous child has great joy; a man who fathers a wise son rejoices in him. May your father and mother rejoice; may she who gave you birth be joyful!

Saying 18: (verses 26-28)

My son, give me your heart and let your eyes delight in my ways, for an adulterous woman is a deep pit, and a wayward wife is a narrow well. Like a bandit she lies in wait and multiplies the unfaithful among men.

Saying 19: (verses 29-35)

Who has woe? Who has sorrow? Who has strife? Who has complaints? Who has needless bruises? Who has bloodshot eyes? Those who linger over wine, who go to sample bowls of mixed wine. Do not gaze at wine when it is red, when it sparkles in the cup, when it goes down smoothly! In the end it bites like a snake and poisons like a viper. Your eyes will see strange sights, and your mind will imagine confusing things. You will be like one sleeping on the high seas, lying on top of the rigging. "They hit me," you will say, "but I'm not hurt! They beat me, but I don't feel it! When will I wake up so I can find another drink?"

Chapter 24

Locked, Loaded and Eligible... Picked Last

"So the last will be first, and the first will be last."
(Matthew 20:16)

ESPN Rebirth Documentary Video

"Locked, Loaded and Eligible...Picked Last" Narrative

As if finally playing football again after two years on the sidelines wasn't incentive enough, as if the 2017 UAB football team needed any additional motivation, it arrived in the form of a most unflattering preseason prediction.

There were 130 teams in 2017 in the Football Bowl Subdivision. SB Nation, using Bill Connelly's respected S&P+ projections, ranked the teams in February from 1-130.

Alabama was ranked No. 1. At the other end of the spectrum, just an hour away on Interstate-65, UAB was picked No. 130. Put another way, the Blazers were expected to be the worst team in the country.

Those projections were based on three reasonable factors: recent history, returning production, and recruiting. To be fair, UAB hadn't played the last two years and its recruiting was a mix of faith and hope.

What those projections didn't measure, what they couldn't measure, was UAB coach Bill Clark's history as a winner and his staff's ability to find quality football players ready, willing, and able to take advantage of a second chance.

Some things can't be measured or projected accurately with metrics and analytics. Clark didn't stick around through the uncertain months of 2015 and the trying times of 2016 to coach the worst team in the country in 2017. He and his players had a much different plan in mind.

Documentary

"Preview 2017: CFN Rankings No. 1-130"

"Locked, Loaded and Eligible...Picked Last"

Chapter 24 Worship Song
Lecrae - "TELL THE WORLD" Feat. Mali Music

What is your, or someone you know, best story of going from counted out to high on the list and or victorious?

Explain.

What applicable principle can you learn and apply from this observation?

Prayer: *Dear God it's not where we start that matters, but where we finish...Father,*

Lesson 24 Coaching Point:

You must believe God can take you from anywhere to anywhere He wants to.

Joel Osteen Video Message
"Right On Time"

Read Proverbs 24 (NIV) and highlight the phrases that speak to your heart:

Wise Sayings from Proverbs 24

Saying 20: (verses 1-2)

Do not envy the wicked, do not desire their company; for their hearts plot violence, and their lips talk about making trouble.

Saying 21: (verses 3-4)

By wisdom a house is built, and through understanding it is established; through knowledge its rooms are filled with rare and beautiful treasures.

Saying 22: (verses 5-6)

The wise prevail through great power, and those who have knowledge muster their strength. Surely you need guidance to wage war, and victory is won through many advisers.

Saying 23: (verse 7)

Wisdom is too high for fools; in the assembly at the gate they must not open their mouths.

Saying 24: (verses 8-9)

Whoever plots evil will be known as a schemer. The schemes of folly are sin, and people detest a mocker.

Saying 25: (verses 10-12)

If you falter in a time of trouble, how small is your strength! Rescue those being led away to death; hold back those staggering toward slaughter. If you say, "But we knew nothing about this," does not he who weighs the heart perceive it? Does not he who guards your life know it? Will he not repay everyone according to what they have done?

Saying 26: (verses 13-14)

Eat honey, my son, for it is good; honey from the comb is sweet to your taste. Know also that wisdom is like honey for you: If you find it, there is a future hope for you, and your hope will not be cut off.

Saying 27: (verses 15-16)

Do not lurk like a thief near the house of the righteous, do not plunder their dwelling place; for though the righteous fall seven times, they rise again, but the wicked stumble when calamity strikes.

Saying 28: (verses 17-18)

Do not gloat when your enemy falls; when they stumble, do not let your heart rejoice, or the LORD will see and disapprove and turn his wrath away from them.

Saying 29: (verses 19-20)

Do not fret because of evildoers or be envious of the wicked, for the evildoer has no future hope and the lamp of the wicked will be snuffed out.

Saying 30: (verses 21-22)

Fear the LORD and the king, my son, and do not join with rebellious officials, for those two will send sudden destruction on them, and who knows what calamities they can bring?

Further Sayings of the Wise (verses 23-34)

These also are sayings of the wise: To show partiality in judging is not good: Whoever says to the guilty, "You are innocent," will be cursed by peoples and denounced by nations. But it will go well with those who convict the guilty, and rich blessing will come on them.

An honest answer is like a kiss on the lips.

Put your outdoor work in order and get your fields ready; after that, build your house.

Do not testify against your neighbor without cause-would you use your lips to mislead? Do not say, "I'll do to them as they have done to me; I'll pay them back for what they did."

I went past the field of a sluggard, past the vineyard of someone who has no sense; thorns had come up everywhere, the ground was covered with weeds, and the stone wall was in ruins. I applied my heart to what I observed and learned a lesson from what I saw: A little sleep, a little slumber, a little folding of the hands to rest-and poverty will come on you like a thief and scarcity like an armed man.

Chapter 25

House Party

Goes home. Then he calls his friends and neighbors together and says, 'Rejoice with me; I have found my lost sheep.' I tell you that in the same way there will be more rejoicing in heaven over one sinner who repents than over ninety-nine righteous persons who do not need to repent. (Luke 15:6-7)

Sam Hunt UAB Benefit Concert Video

"House Party" Narrative

The first time around when Sam Hunt played for UAB, the Blazers simply weren't very good. His first year in 2006, after transferring from Middle Tennessee, was Watson Brown's last year as head coach. Hunt's last year in 2007 was Neil Callaway's debut. Combined record for those two seasons: 5-19 overall.

It was a sad song on repeat.

The quarterback went on to bigger and better things after his playing days as a country music singer-songwriter. It wouldn't be an exaggeration to call him a star. Meanwhile, the UAB program continued down the bumpy back roads of major college football.

When Hunt returned to Birmingham to play for UAB, to perform a free concert the night before the 2017 season opener against Alabama A&M, he and his old school both had reasons to rejoice. Evidence of their shared enthusiasm was all around them in the Uptown entertainment district. A raucous crowd estimated at 25,000 people showed up to sing along, dance, and revel in the spirit of rebirth.

That year, Billboard picked "Take Your Time" as its favorite Sam Hunt song. That night, he and his team were together again under much more enjoyable circumstances. Their time was now.

Documentaries

"Sam Hunt blazes with good cheer, celebrates return of UAB football with 25,000 fans"

2017 Hype Video

"House Party"

Chapter 25 Worship Song

Crystal Yates Micah Tyler Joshua Sherman "What Mercy Did For Me"

What makes you, or someone you know, throw a party? Explain.

What applicable principle can you learn and apply from this observation?

Prayer: *Dear God when someone or something returns after being gone it is time to celebrate Your unbelievable goodness...Father,*

_____

_____

_____

Lesson 25 Coaching Point:
You must believe God celebrates victories.

Read Proverbs 25 (NIV) and highlight the phrases that speak to your heart:

These are more proverbs of Solomon, compiled by the men of Hezekiah king of Judah: It is the glory of God to conceal a matter; to search out a matter is the glory of kings. As the heavens are high and the earth is deep, so the hearts of kings are unsearchable. Remove the dross from the silver, and a silversmith can produce a vessel; remove wicked officials from the king's presence, and his throne will be established through righteousness. Do not exalt yourself in the king's presence, and do not claim a place among his great men; it is better for him to say to you, "Come up here," than for him to humiliate you before his nobles. What you have seen with your eyes do not bring hastily to court, for what will you do in the end if your neighbor puts you to shame? If you take your neighbor to court, do not betray another's confidence, or the one who hears it may shame you and the charge against you will stand. Like apples of gold in settings of silver is a ruling rightly given. Like an earring of gold or an ornament of fine gold is the rebuke of a wise judge to a listening ear. Like a snow-cooled drink at harvest time is a trustworthy messenger to the one who sends him; he refreshes the spirit of his master. Like clouds and wind without rain is one who boasts of gifts never given. Through patience a ruler can be persuaded, and a gentle tongue can break a bone. If you find honey, eat just enough-too much of it, and you will vomit. Seldom set foot in your neighbor's house-too much of you, and they will hate you. Like a club or a sword or a sharp arrow is one who gives false testimony against a neighbor. Like a broken tooth or a lame foot is reliance on the unfaithful in a time of trouble. Like one who takes away a garment on a cold day, or like vinegar poured on a wound, is one who sings songs to a heavy heart. If your enemy is hungry, give him food to eat; if he is thirsty, give him water to drink. In doing this, you will heap burning coals on his head, and the LORD will reward you. Like a north wind that brings unexpected rain is a sly tongue-which provokes a horrified look. Better to live on a corner of the roof than share a house with a quarrelsome wife. Like cold water to a weary soul is good news from a distant land. Like a muddied spring or a polluted well are the righteous who give way to the wicked. It is not good to eat too much honey, nor is it honorable to search out matters that are too deep. Like a city whose walls are broken through is a person who lacks self-control. (Proverbs 25)

Chapter 26

The City Rejoices...
The Return...Kickoff

When the righteous prosper, the city rejoices; when the wicked perish, there are shouts of joy. Through the blessing of the upright a city is exalted, but by the mouth of the wicked it is destroyed. (Proverbs 11:10-11)

Together We are Greater Birmingham Video

"The City Rejoices" Narrative

The first game of every football season is cause for celebration, especially in the Deep South, but there may never be another season-opener quite like the one Legion Field hosted on September 2, 2017. It wasn't just the start of another year for UAB. It was a new beginning for the city of Birmingham.

It had been 1,008 days since the Blazers had played a game. Not a spring game. Not a scrimmage game. An honest-to-goodness college football game. It had been two years, nine months, and four days of despair replaced by hope, anger forged into determination, and anticipation motivated by the teamwork of an entire city.

The final score-UAB 38, Alabama A&M 7-doesn't begin to tell the story. On that day, #TheReturn was no longer just a catchy slogan made into a hashtag. It was a reality, a living, breathing, smiling, satisfying reality. This was the day so many people in Birmingham had fought for, and it attracted the largest crowd in school history-45,212 strong.

When Tim Alexander, the emotional leader of the fight to revive the program, stood from his wheelchair to deliver the game ball at midfield, it was a metaphor and a moment overflowing with meaning. The Blazers were back on their feet because you can't keep a good man, or a great community, down.

Documentary: "UAB back in action, Blazers community ready for an exciting season"

"The City Rejoices"

Chapter 26 Worship Song
Todd Dulaney "Victory Belongs To Jesus"

What is your, or someone you know, favorite City or Town and why?

Explain.

What applicable principle can you learn and apply from this observation?

Prayer: *Dear God, we become the people that we live with so friends, community and city are critical...Father,*

_____

_____

_____

Lesson 26 Coaching Point:
You must believe God will bless the peoples that bless Him.

Joel Osteen Video Message
"Knowing You Are Loved"

Read Proverbs 26 (NIV) and highlight the phrases that speak to your heart:

Like snow in summer or rain in harvest, honor is not fitting for a fool. Like a fluttering sparrow or a darting swallow, an undeserved curse does not come to rest. A whip for the horse, a bridle for the donkey, and a rod for the backs of fools! Do not answer a fool according to his folly, or you yourself will be just like him. Answer a fool according to his folly, or he will be wise in his own eyes. Sending a message by the hands of a fool is like cutting off one's feet or drinking poison. Like the useless legs of one who is lame is a proverb in the mouth of a fool. Like tying a stone in a sling is the giving of honor to a fool. Like a thorn bush in a drunkard's hand is a proverb in the mouth of a fool. Like an archer who wounds at random is one who hires a fool or any passer-by. As a dog returns to its vomit, so fools repeat their folly. Do you see a person wise in their own eyes? There is more hope for a fool than for them. A sluggard says, "There's a lion in the road, a fierce lion roaming the streets!" As a door turns on its hinges, so a sluggard turns on his bed. A sluggard buries his hand in the dish; he is too lazy to bring it back to his mouth. A sluggard is wiser in his own eyes than seven people who answer discreetly. Like one who grabs a stray dog by the ears is someone who rushes into a quarrel not their own. Like a maniac shooting flaming arrows of death is one who deceives their neighbor and says, "I was only joking!" Without wood a fire goes out; without a gossip a quarrel dies down. As charcoal to embers and as wood to fire, so is a quarrelsome person for kindling strife. The words of a gossip are like choice morsels; they go down to the inmost parts. Like a coating of silver dross on earthenware are fervent lips with an evil heart. Enemies disguise themselves with their lips, but in their hearts they harbor deceit. Though their speech is charming, do not believe them, for seven abominations fill their hearts. Their malice may be concealed by deception, but their wickedness will be exposed in the assembly. Whoever digs a pit will fall into it; if someone rolls a stone, it will roll back on them. A lying tongue hates those it hurts, and a flattering mouth works ruin. (Proverbs 26)

Games 1-6 and Homecoming for the Children

At that time the disciples came to Jesus and asked, "Who, then, is the greatest in the kingdom of heaven?" He called a little child to him, and placed the child among them. And he said: "Truly I tell you, unless you change and become like little children, you will never enter the kingdom of heaven. Therefore, whoever takes the lowly position of this child is the greatest in the kingdom of heaven. And whoever welcomes one such child in my name welcomes me. (Matthew 18:1-5)

Children's Harbor Documentary Video

"Games 1-6 and Homecoming for the Children" Narrative

Coach Bill Clark has a Pyramid for Success with three fundamental rules for everyone in his program: "Protect the Team; Be Ready; and No Excuses." The Blazers continued to follow those rules as they moved beyond the exhilaration of their opening victory.

A pattern developed during the first half of the season. UAB found strength at home and struggle on the road, splitting its first four games. Then came a homecoming for the ages, a vivid reminder of the special bond between a football team and its community.

Against Conference USA contender Louisiana Tech, the unselfish Blazers played for the names on the back of their jerseys - because those names belonged to the seriously ill patients of Children's Harbor, which provides youngsters and their families a no-cost place to get away from their hospital stays.

Embracing the little children as Jesus instructed lifted the Blazers. They soared to block La Tech's potential game-winning field goal on the final play. It was a sign that something special was happening here, but it didn't end there.

The next week, UAB upset C-USA power Middle Tennessee, which had beaten the Syracuse team that would take down defending national champion Clemson. That surprise put the

165

Blazers at 4-2 at the midpoint of the regular season. They were becoming a legitimate football team as well as a heartwarming story.

Documentary

"Recapping the First Half of UABs Historic 2017 Season"

"Games 1-6 and Homecoming for the Children"

Chapter 27 Worship Song
Lecrae-Tori Kelly "I'll Find You"

What is a valuable lesson that you, or someone you know, have learned from a child at some point in your life?

Explain.

What applicable principle can you learn and apply from this observation?

Prayer: *Dear God, I know that You love children and child-like faith...Father,*

_____

_____

_____

Lesson 27 Coaching Point:
You must believe God expects and rewards child like faith.

Steven Furtick Video Message
"He's Doing A New Thing"

Read Proverbs 27 (NIV) and highlight the phrases that speak to your heart:

Do not boast about tomorrow, for you do not know what a day may bring. Let someone else praise you, and not your own mouth; an outsider, and not your own lips. Stone is heavy and sand a burden, but a fool's provocation is heavier than both. Anger is cruel and fury overwhelming, but who can stand before jealousy? Better is open rebuke than hidden love. Wounds from a friend can be trusted, but an enemy multiplies kisses. One who is full loathes honey from the comb, but to the hungry even what is bitter tastes sweet. Like a bird that flees its nest is anyone who flees from home. Perfume and incense bring joy to the heart, and the pleasantness of a friend springs from their heartfelt advice. Do not forsake your friend or a friend of your family, and do not go to your relative's house when disaster strikes you-better a neighbor nearby than a relative far away. Be wise, my son, and bring joy to my heart; then I can answer anyone who treats me with contempt. The prudent see danger and take refuge, but the simple keep going and pay the penalty. Take the garment of one who puts up security for a stranger; hold it in pledge if it is done for an outsider. If anyone loudly blesses their neighbor early in the morning, it will be taken as a curse. A quarrelsome wife is like the dripping of a leaky roof in a rainstorm; restraining her is like restraining the wind or grasping oil with the hand. As iron sharpens iron, so one person sharpens another. The one who guards a fig tree will eat its fruit, and whoever protects their master will be honored. As water reflects the face, so one's life reflects the heart. Death and Destruction are never satisfied, and neither are human eyes. The crucible for silver and the furnace for gold, but people are tested by their praise. Though you grind a fool in a mortar, grinding them like grain with a pestle, you will not remove their folly from them. Be sure you know the condition of your flocks, give careful attention to your herds; for riches do not endure forever, and a crown is not secure for all generations. When the hay is removed and new growth appears and the grass from the hills is gathered in, the lambs will provide you with clothing, and the goats with the price of a field. You will have plenty of goats' milk to feed your family and to nourish your female servants. (Proverbs 27)

Chapter 28

Games 7-12
Finishing What We Brought Back

Therefore, since we are surrounded by such a cloud of witnesses, let us throw off everything that hinders and the sin that so easily entangles. And let us run with perseverance the race marked out for us, fixing our eyes on Jesus, the pioneer and perfecter of faith. For the joy set before him he endured the cross, scorning its shame, and sat down at the right hand of the throne of God. Consider him who endured such opposition from sinners, so that you will not grow weary and lose heart. (Hebrews 12:1-3)

6-0 at Home Video

"Games 7-12 Finishing What We Brought Back" Narrative

Reality set in again as the Blazers returned to the road. Charlotte was winless through seven games. Charlotte was supposed to be an easy mark for UAB's first win away from home. Charlotte didn't cooperate, handing the Blazers a heartbreaking overtime defeat with a two-point conversion that shocked and rocked the upstarts, making them question their ability to ever win a road game.

The very next week, the schedule sent them to rival Southern Miss. It was the place where UAB had won its final game before the 2014 shutdown in resounding fashion, and it would be the place where the new UAB would prove itself more than capable away from Birmingham with a three-touchdown victory.

Winning was now a habit regardless of location. A home win against Rice made the Blazers bowl-eligible. A road win at UTSA was victory No. 7, matching the program's Football Bowl Subdivision high. A final home triumph against UTEP kept them undefeated at Legion Field and lifted them to 8-4 overall, setting a new school FBS record for victories in a single season.

For the second time in school history, UAB was headed to a bowl game. Earning that Bahamas Bowl bid, in the year of #TheReturn, made this truly a season for all time.

Documentary: "In leading resurrected UAB to a bowl, no coach compared to Bill Clark in 2017"

"Games 7-12 Finishing What We Brought Back"

Chapter 28 Worship Song

Tauren Wells – "Hills and Valleys"

Have you, or someone you know, ever had a bad experience that you feel like prepared you as a person to do something more significant later?

Explain.

What applicable principle can you learn and apply from this observation?

Prayer: *Dear God, I know that there are a lot of people cheering us on earth as well as in heaven...Father,*

_____

_____

_____

Lesson 28 Coaching Point:

You must believe God provides you with Jesus' example to endure anything to the finish.

Craig Groeschel Video Message
<u>"Forgiving God-The Grudge"</u>

Read Proverbs 28 (NIV) and highlight the phrases that speak to your heart:

The wicked flee though no one pursues, but the righteous are as bold as a lion. When a country is rebellious, it has many rulers, but a ruler with discernment and knowledge maintains order. A ruler who oppresses the poor is like a driving rain that leaves no crops. Those who forsake instruction praise the wicked, but those who heed it resist them. Evildoers do not understand what is right, but those who seek the LORD understand it fully. Better the poor whose walk is blameless than the rich whose ways are perverse. A discerning son heeds instruction, but a companion of gluttons disgraces his father. Whoever increases wealth by taking interest or profit from the poor amasses it for another, who will be kind to the poor. If anyone turns a deaf ear to my instruction, even their prayers are detestable. Whoever leads the upright along an evil path will fall into their own trap, but the blameless will receive a good inheritance. The rich are wise in their own eyes; one who is poor and discerning sees how deluded they are. When the righteous triumph, there is great elation; but when the wicked rise to power, people go into hiding. Whoever conceals their sins does not prosper, but the one who confesses and renounces them finds mercy. Blessed is the one who always trembles before God, but whoever hardens their heart falls into trouble. Like a roaring lion or a charging bear is a wicked ruler over a helpless people. A tyrannical ruler practices extortion, but one who hates ill-gotten gain will enjoy a long reign. Anyone tormented by the guilt of murder will seek refuge in the grave; let no one hold them back. The one whose walk is blameless is kept safe, but the one whose ways are perverse will fall into the pit. Those who work their land will have abundant food, but those who chase fantasies will have their fill of poverty. A faithful person will be richly blessed, but one eager to get rich will not go unpunished. To show partiality is not good-yet a person will do wrong for a piece of bread. The stingy are eager to get rich and are unaware that poverty awaits them. Whoever rebukes a person will in the end gain favor rather than one who has a flattering tongue. Whoever robs their father or mother and says, "It's not wrong," is partner to one who destroys. The greedy stir up conflict, but those who trust in the LORD *will prosper. Those who trust in themselves are fools, but those who walk in wisdom are kept safe. Those who give to the poor will lack nothing, but those who close their eyes to them receive many curses. When the wicked rise to power, people go into hiding; but when the wicked perish, the righteous thrive.* (Proverbs 28)

The Bahamas Bowl and Looking Beyond

For I know the plans I have for you," declares the LORD, "plans to prosper you and not to harm you, plans to give you hope and a future. (Jeremiah 29:11)

Comeback Recap Video

"The Bahamas Bowl and Looking Beyond" Narrative

By any measure, the 2017 UAB football season was a success long before the Blazers kicked off to Ohio University in the Bahamas Bowl. Simply getting back on the field at all was a triumph, but the results? The records? The memories? They were exceedingly, abundantly more than anyone involved in the program could've asked or imagined.

An undefeated home record was a return on the community's investment. A program FBS single-season record of eight wins and the second bowl bid in school history were tangible evidence of what was possible. Those accomplishments resonated even more because they were achieved in the first year back on the field after two years of hard work to make #TheReturn a reality.

The Bahamas Bowl itself showed there was much more work to do. That game was a classic case of one team that was happy to be there against an opponent that was there to make something happen. Ohio scored a touchdown on the opening possession and didn't let up. UAB played as if it were on vacation after its tremendous season.

The 41-6 battering was just the medicine the Blazers needed to motivate them during the off-season to come, to fuel them to reach even greater heights, and write more memorable chapters. You could knock them down for a day, but the world had learned something about these players and coaches. Nothing would keep them down, not after that season.

Documentary

"Bahamas Bowl: UAB loses to Ohio 41-6"

"The Bahamas Bowl and Looking Beyond"

Chapter 29 Worship Song
Hillsong Worship "Who You Say I Am"

What is your, or someone that you know, hope for the future? Explain.

What applicable principle can you learn and apply from this observation?

Prayer: *Dear God, when You are in the beginning then I can rest assured the end results are going to be good...Father,*

_____

_____

_____

Lesson 29 Coaching Point:

You must believe God loves you and His plans are for your prosperity.

Steven Furtick Video Message
<u>"Stop Waiting For It; Walk In It"</u>

Read Proverbs 29 (NIV) and highlight the phrases that speak to your heart:

Whoever remains stiff-necked after many rebukes will suddenly be destroyed-without remedy. When the righteous thrive, the people rejoice; when the wicked rule, the people groan. A man who loves wisdom brings joy to his father, but a companion of prostitutes squanders his wealth. By justice a king gives a country stability, but those who are greedy for bribes tear it down. Those who flatter their neighbors are spreading nets for their feet. Evildoers are snared by their own sin, but the righteous shout for joy and are glad. The righteous care about justice for the poor, but the wicked have no such concern. Mockers stir up a city, but the wise turn away anger. If a wise person goes to court with a fool, the fool rages and scoffs, and there is no peace. The bloodthirsty hate a person of integrity and seek to kill the upright. Fools give full vent to their rage, but the wise bring calm in the end. If a ruler listens to lies, all his officials become wicked. The poor and the oppressor have this in common: The LORD gives sight to the eyes of both. If a king judges the poor with fairness, his throne will be established forever. A rod and a reprimand impart wisdom, but a child left undisciplined disgraces its mother. When the wicked thrive, so does sin, but the righteous will see their downfall. Discipline your children, and they will give you peace; they will bring you the delights you desire. Where there is no revelation, people cast off restraint; but blessed is the one who heeds wisdom's instruction. Servants cannot be corrected by mere words; though they understand, they will not respond. Do you see someone who speaks in haste? There is more hope for a fool than for them. A servant pampered from youth will turn out to be insolent. An angry person stirs up conflict, and a hot-tempered person commits many sins. Pride brings a person low, but the lowly in spirit gain honor. The accomplices of thieves are their own enemies; they are put under oath and dare not testify. Fear of man will prove to be a snare, but whoever trusts in the Lord *is kept safe. Many seek an audience with a ruler, but it is from the* Lord *that one gets justice. The righteous detest the dishonest; the wicked detest the upright.* (Proverbs 29)

2018-19 Regular Seasons...Wow

Not only so, but we also glory in our sufferings, because we know that suffering produces perseverance; perseverance, character; and character, hope. And hope does not put us to shame, because God's love has been poured out into our hearts through the Holy Spirit, who has been given to us. (Romans 5:3-5)

Greatest Show On Earth Video

"2018-19 Regular Seasons...Wow" Narrative

The dawn of the two seasons to follow simply meant different doubts and questions, and the Blazers heard them all. Nice story, but you won in 2017 because you snuck up on people. Buckle up because now you'll be circled on other people's schedules. In 2018 it was, "We'll see how you handle these elevated expectations. Won't be so easy this year." Then in 2019, "Okay, yeah, two good years with all those JUCO kids that you got in, but 30+ graduated and the bottom may fall out."

UAB Head Coach Bill Clark had the perfect response to that noise when he said, "We have a pen, too. We can circle them right back. We didn't stop recruiting when we got all those good players in and we have some pretty good young guys following."

The message: There would be no complacency in this program. To put the critics to rest, the Blazers had to aim higher, dig deeper, work harder than ever to show that 2017 wasn't a fluke. It was only the beginning.

And so they did. Birmingham's team was nothing short of magical in the Magic City for the next two years, building a home-field winning streak that ranked among the best in the country, posting monstrous Legion Field wins over Tulane and North Texas. With the exception of an early loss at Coastal Carolina, they handled their business away from home, too. In 2018, they started 8-1 overall to give themselves a chance to do something UAB football had never done...beat rival Southern Miss at home, and they would clinch the Conference USA Western Division title and a spot in the C-USA Championship Game. History was in their grasp. In 2019, the home streak continued to 18-0. Call it magic, call it special, whatever you call it Birmingham and Legion Field have a supernatural relationship with the Blazers.

Documentary

<u>"UAB's Bill Clark is Sporting News' 2018 Coach of the Year"</u>

"2018-19 Regular Seasons...Wow"

Chapter 30 Worship Song
Lacrea "Go Hard"

What suffering have you, or someone you know, endured in life that later manifested itself in a character quality needed?

Explain.

What applicable principle can you learn and apply from this observation?

Prayer: *Dear God, I know that we become strong by enduring trials and leaning on hope in You...Father,*

_____

_____

_____

Lesson 30 Coaching Point:

You must believe God allows trials to develop you into your best self.

Craig Groeschel Video Message
"Selfless - Grateful In The Grind"

Read Proverbs 30 (NIV) and highlight the phrases that speak to your heart:

The sayings of Agur son of Jakeh-an inspired utterance. This man's utterance to Ithiel: "I am weary, God, but I can prevail. Surely I am only a brute, not a man; I do not have human understanding. I have not learned wisdom, nor have I attained to the knowledge of the Holy One. Who has gone up to heaven and come down? Whose hands have gathered up the wind? Who has wrapped up the waters in a cloak? Who has established all the ends of the earth? What is his name, and what is the name of his son? Surely you know! "Every word of God is flawless; he is a shield to those who take refuge in him. Do not add to his words, or he will rebuke you and prove you a liar. "Two things I ask of you, LORD; do not refuse me before I die: Keep falsehood and lies far from me; give me neither poverty nor riches, but give me only my daily bread. Otherwise, I may have too much and disown you and say, 'Who is the LORD?' Or I may become poor and steal, and so dishonor the name of my God. "Do not slander a servant to their master, or they will curse you, and you will pay for it. "There are those who curse their fathers and do not bless their mothers; those who are pure in their own eyes and yet are not cleansed of their filth; those whose eyes are ever so haughty, whose glances are so disdainful; those whose teeth are swords and whose jaws are set with knives to devour the poor from the earth and the needy from among mankind. "The leech has two daughters. 'Give! Give!' they cry. "There are three things that are never satisfied, four that never say, 'Enough!': the grave, the barren womb, land, which is never satisfied with water, and fire, which never says, 'Enough!' "The eye that mocks a father, that scorns an aged mother, will be pecked out by the ravens of the valley, will be eaten by the vultures. "There are three things that are too amazing for me, four that I do not understand: the way of an eagle in the sky, the way of a snake on a rock, the way of a ship on the high seas, and the way of a man with a young woman. "This is the way of an adulterous woman: She eats and wipes her mouth and says, 'I've done nothing wrong.' "Under three things the earth trembles under four it cannot bear up: a servant who becomes king, a godless fool who gets plenty to eat, a contemptible woman who gets married, and a servant who displaces her mistress. "Four things on earth are small, yet they are extremely wise: Ants are creatures of little strength, yet they store up their food in the summer; hyraxes are creatures of little power, yet they make their home in the crags; locusts have no king, yet they advance together in ranks; a lizard can be caught with the hand, yet it is found in kings' palaces. "There are three things that are stately in their stride, four that move with stately bearing: a lion, mighty among beasts, who retreats before nothing; a strutting rooster, a he-goat, and a king secure against revolt. "If you play the fool and exalt yourself, or if you plan evil, clap your hand over your mouth! For as churning cream produces butter, and as twisting the nose produces blood, so stirring up anger produces strife." (Proverbs 30)

Chapter 31

2018-19 Championship Seasons...Wow

But those who hope in the LORD will renew their strength. They will soar on wings like eagles; they will run and not grow weary, they will walk and not be faint. (Isaiah 40:31)

2019 West Championship Game Highlights

"2018-19 Championship Seasons...Wow" Narrative

After clinching the West in 2018, the Blazers took to the road to win the whole shooting match against MTSU in Murfreesboro. First the final regular season game which UAB lost in embarrassing fashion cost the Blazers the championship game home field advantage the very next Saturday. However, with their iron clad character forged in the furnaces of the past, the resurrection team turned around the next Saturday and won the championship game with a field goal in the end back at MTSU's home.

With the Bahamas Bowl loss fresh on their mind, the Blazers were ready to head back south and settle unfinished business. A loss was not an option this time. With an electrifying and determined mindset, Coach Clark and the Blazers set off to Boca Raton to claim what was theirs. A sense of pride, respect, rings, and another chance to make history was on the line. The only thing standing in their way was the Northern Illinois University Huskies football team. End result 37-13 UAB.

Then as an encore in 2019, the Blazer team, allegedly depleted of all relevant talent, proceeded to win the C-USA West division and head back to Boca Raton, Florida to face a Lane Kiffin coached Florida Atlantic University East Championship team for an unprecedented repeat C-USA Championship two years in a row on the road. No visiting team had ever won a C-USA championship before UAB did it in 2018. The Blazers were beaten in that championship game by the Kiffin coached team as he headed to Ole Miss as their new head coach. The Blazers then took to the

189

New Orleans Bowl and fought valiantly against #20 Appalachian State only to fall short in the end but as you now know, the Blazers have been down before only to rise again.

The miracles continued and continue. However, somewhere we have to stop writing, and put a bow on this story, so that is what we are doing now in 2020. History is written and still yet to write.

Documentaries

"Just 2 years after program's restart, UAB beats Northern Illinois for first bowl win ever"

"Rewinding UAB's 31-17 loss in the New Orleans Bowl"

The Best of College Football (Bowl Games)

"2018-19 Championship Seasons...Wow "

Chapter 31 Worship Song
Newsboys – "Greatness Of Our God"

Have you, or someone you know, ever been told that you couldn't do something, but you were determined and did it anyway?

Explain.

What applicable principle can you learn and apply from this observation?

Prayer: *Dear God my strength comes from my hope in You and that hope renews...Father,*

_____

_____

_____

Lesson 31 Coaching Point:

You must believe God gives you hope which will renew your strength and take you to higher successes.

Steven Furtick Video Message
"The Paradox Of Progress"

Read Proverbs 31 (NIV) and highlight the phrases that speak to your heart:

The sayings of King Lemuel-an inspired utterance his mother taught him. Listen, my son! Listen, son of my womb! Listen, my son, the answer to my prayers! Do not spend your strength[a] on women, your vigor on those who ruin kings. It is not for kings, Lemuel-it is not for kings to drink wine, not for rulers to crave beer, lest they drink and forget what has been decreed, and deprive all the oppressed of their rights. Let beer be for those who are perishing, wine for those who are in anguish! Let them drink and forget their poverty and remember their misery no more. Speak up for those who cannot speak for themselves, for the rights of all who are destitute. Speak up and judge fairly; defend the rights of the poor and needy. A wife of noble character who can find? She is worth far more than rubies. Her husband has full confidence in her and lacks nothing of value. She brings him good, not harm, all the days of her life. She selects wool and flax and works with eager hands. She is like the merchant ships, bringing her food from afar. She gets up while it is still night; she provides food for her family and portions for her female servants. She considers a field and buys it; out of her earnings she plants a vineyard. She sets about her work vigorously; her arms are strong for her tasks. She sees that her trading is profitable, and her lamp does not go out at night. In her hand she holds the distaff and grasps the spindle with her fingers. She opens her arms to the poor and extends her hands to the needy. When it snows, she has no fear for her household; for all of them are clothed in scarlet. She makes coverings for her bed; she is clothed in fine linen and purple. Her husband is respected at the city gate, where he takes his seat among the elders of the land. She makes linen garments and sells them, and supplies the merchants with sashes. She is clothed with strength and dignity; she can laugh at the days to come. She speaks with wisdom, and faithful instruction is on her tongue. She watches over the affairs of her household and does not eat the bread of idleness. Her children arise and call her blessed; her husband also, and he praises her: "Many women do noble things, but you surpass them all." Charm is deceptive, and beauty is fleeting; but a woman who fears the LORD is to be praised. Honor her for all that her hands have done, and let her works bring her praise at the city gate. (Proverbs 31)

Chapter 32

Resurrection Story to be Continued... Worldwide...You In?

Very truly I tell you, whoever believes in me will do the works I have been doing, and they will do even greater things than these, because I am going to the Father. (John 14:12)

2019 UAB Football Video...Story to be Continued

"Resurrection Story to be Continued... Worldwide...You In?" Narrative

T he return of UAB football illustrates a lot of what goes on in the hearts, minds and souls of a southern man destined to find their God given star-power in the game of football. What a great story **it** is, but UAB and these other stories in this book are just a few.

As this book is being published, the 2019 football season has ended but the future is still being written. UAB lost 30+ seniors from the 2018 C-USA Championship team and the doubters were out in force but the Blazers stretched their undefeated Legion Field record to 18-0, won 9 games and played in the third straight bowl game since the return. 2020 welcomes 18 starters back and the future looks brighter than ever.

Coach Clark leads the team in a daily mantra that says: We are family. We never quit. We make history. We are UAB...Champs on 3...1-2-3...CHAMPS!

We truly are all family because of the shared experiences we have had unlike any others.

We never quit as demonstrated through the fire time and time again over the course of the last 5 years since the beginning of the return. Indeed, we have made history and yes, we are champions.

Absolutely, we/ UAB is a unique institution of higher education geographically situated at the epicenter of where football is important. Many of the players have come and scattered abroad once again, some to their homes and some to destinations

195

elsewhere. Character has been forged through the fire and lives have been changed. The great thing is the changes can be paid forward to generations to come.

We have only scratched the surface of what really goes on inside the heart and soul of a southern man with some of these stories. The best stories you or I will never know.

Most of the greatest moments in sports originate from the depths of one's spirit and are known only by God and that one person, but sometimes God decides to change the world with a public display of a few of those great moments that come from Deep in the Heart.

Documentary
"Is it really possible for Christians to do greater works than Jesus?"

2020 UAB Football Schedule...Story to be Continued

"Resurrection Story to be Continued... Worldwide...You In?"

Chapter 32 Worship Song

<u>Lauren Daigle - "You Say"</u>

What could you do in your own personal life that in perspective would be even greater than some of the miracles that Jesus performed? Explain.

What applicable principle can you learn and apply from this observation?

Prayer: *Dear God, I can do all things through Christ who strengthens me. The most powerful force in the universe lives in us and works through us...Father,*

_____

_____

_____

Lesson 32 Coaching Point:

You must believe God allows you to do all things through Christ who strengthens you.

Craig Groeschel Video Message

"Shut The Door On Distractions"

Chapter 33

Inside These Lines...Can We Resolve Social Unrest?

For if we have been united with him in a death like his, we will certainly also be united with him in a resurrection like his. (Romans 6:5)

Inside These Lines Video

"Inside These Lines…Can We Resolve Social Unrest?" Narrative

D eep in the Heart of Birmingham, Alabama, the South and this great nation of ours a story of enthusiasm for good manifests itself in the resurrection of a college football program.

As someone that has been blessed to arrive at the UAB football office the day after the reinstatement of the program in 2015 and be a part of the entire process while watching #TheReturn happen, I have seen a microcosm within the program of what people want and need in the real world. Can that same passionate spirit somehow be channeled to unify other campuses, communities, cites, states, the nation, and the world? Can we acknowledge our differences while embracing our humanity?

In the arena of unity as Romans 6:5 states, it of course all starts and finishes with Jesus. "For if we have been united with him in a death like his, we will certainly also be united with him in a resurrection like his."

My life verse says in Colossians 1:17: "He is before all things, and in Him **all things are held together.**" I have always followed that verse with the thought that then we can only assume that without Jesus all things that aren't held together are going to fall apart.

Everything falling apart without Jesus has been my observation and one of the main takeaways that I have gotten out of this life.

And if the Spirit of Him who raised Jesus from the dead is living in you, that Spirit can bring a person, a family, a team, a university, a city, a state, a country, or a world back to life from **Deep in the Heart**.

Even as we speak, there are protests in various cities around the country pitting Conservatives against Liberals, Christians against Muslims, Homosexuals against Heterosexuals, and Race against Race just to name a few.

What we need to focus on is not what we are against, but what we are for, knowing that we are all children of the Most High God, qualified for His favor and blessings and that there is only one race, that is the human race.

Much work still to be done on the field and off.

Story to be continued….Stay Tuned for **it**.

Documentary

"Stick to Sports: Why Sports and Politics are the Perfect Mix"

"Inside These Lines...Can We Resolve Social Unrest?"

Chapter 33 Worship Song
Michael W Smith - "Jesus is the Answer"

Have you, or someone you know, ever seen what appeared to be an irresolvable personality conflict be resolved and get new life after?

Explain.

What applicable principle can you learn and apply from this observation?

Prayer: *Dear God, with Jesus in us we are enabled with the power to resurrect and certainly to unite...Father,*

_____

_____

_____

Lesson 33 Coaching Point:

You must believe God through Jesus' resurrection power can solve relational problems.

Steven Furtick Video Message

<u>"The Devil Likes To Twist The Truth"</u>

Epilogue

Who Will Go?

Then I heard the voice of the Lord saying, "Whom shall I send? And who will go for us?" And I said, "Here am I. Send me!" (Isaiah 6:8)

Lacrea - "Send Me I'll Go"

This book could have very well inspired you to want to rise to a new level of faith, but don't let it end there.

Whatever you discovered in this uniquely formatted book and the incredible stories on top of stories, be thinking about how you can act on what you need to in your own personal life. This brings us to two final stories we want to share with you in this epilogue for your meditation and reflection. We want to encourage you with these two stories shared along the football road we've traveled. We share these two stories with you because the Alpha story illustrates part of the reason football is so important. The Omega is a call to action story we should all take to heart.

My Alpha story as told by retired Marine Corps LTC Mark Tingle:

A dear friend of mine was an Infantry Officer in the United States Marine Corps. He thrives on competition and loves American Football. He coached and played, and his daughter was a Punt, Pass and Kick National Finalist. In the fall of 1997, he was given a week-long assignment as a liaison officer for three Russian Generals visiting Camp Lejeune, NC. He was responsible for driving them to briefings, answering any questions, and explaining unfamiliar nuances of the Marine Corps' lexicon. As his week-long assignment came to a close and the generals prepared to return to Russia, they attended a football game. On the drive to the game, fundamentals of the game were explained. About halfway through the second quarter, the Russian Generals chatted quietly among themselves. As my buddy moved closer to the three senior officers, one of them looked at him and asked, "How often do America's youth play this sport?"

"Every Friday night," my friend said.

The general then asked, "Everywhere?"

"Yes, sir. All across America every Friday night in the fall."

"How do they learn?" the general asked.

He received the reply, "America's youth start developing their game skills and competitive spirit in elementary school."

The Russians conferred again before saying, "We never could have won a war then."

Explaining that based on what they were witnessing: the spirit of competition, combined with controlled, interpersonal violence, teamwork, camaraderie, and physical adversity, they believed their country could not be victorious against the United States military.

Our Omega story is one John Maxwell tells about Abraham Lincoln:

President Abraham Lincoln, an incredible communicator, was known during the Civil War to attend a church not far from the White House on Wednesday nights. The preacher, Dr. Gurley, allowed the President to sit in the pastor's study with the door open to the chancel so he could listen to the sermon without having to interact with the crowd.

One Wednesday evening as Lincoln and a companion walked back to the White House after the sermon, the President's companion asked, "What did you think of tonight's sermon?"

"Well," Lincoln responded, "it was brilliantly conceived, biblical, relevant, and well presented."

"So, it was a great sermon?" Lincoln's companion confidently asked.

"No," Lincoln replied. "It failed. It failed because Dr. Gurley did not ask us to do something great."

The point is-as President Lincoln noted above-no matter how biblical, relevant, well presented or even brilliant your message may be, the lack of a clear and compelling call to action will render it a failure in motivating people to radical obedience.

As the late great Zig Ziglar would say, "You have to **do** before you can **be** and you have to **be** before you can **have**." So perhaps you are inspired and ask, "What should I **do** now?"

When Jesus was asked, "What is the most important thing we can **do**?" paraphrased, He replied, "Love God and Love Others." So, quite simply remember this two-letter acronym, **G.O.**, Love God and Others.

In your loving of God and Others, you will be called to **do** a lot of things. Some things God asks you to **do** will be relatively easy and some things God asks you to **do** will be hard.

No matter what, **do** what God tells you to **do** and you will find yourself becoming what you are supposed to **be** and having what you are supposed to **have** which ultimately will cause you to reach the fullness of your destiny from Deep in the Heart.

Reaching the fullness of your destiny is our prayer for you, in Jesus' name.

If you receive **it** say, "Amen."

"Who will go?" Final Devotion

Epilogue Worship Song
<u>Big Daddy Weave - "Overwhelmed"</u>

Have you, or someone you know, ever been on a mission? Explain.

What applicable principle can you learn and apply from this observation?

Prayer: *Dear God, when You say "go," I must just do it knowing that You love me and You are going to take care of me. The operational definition of success is simply obeying You...Father,*

_____

_____

_____

Epilogue Coaching Point:

You must believe God sending you on a mission assures you that you are going to ultimately succeed.

Joel Osteen Video Message

<u>"Just Obey"</u>

The Great Commission

Then the eleven disciples went to Galilee, to the mountain where Jesus had told them to go. When they saw him, they worshiped him; but some doubted. Then Jesus came to them and said, "All authority in heaven and on earth has been given to me. Therefore go and make disciples of all nations, baptizing them in the name of the Father and of the Son and of the Holy Spirit, and teaching them to obey everything I have commanded you. And

surely I am with you always, to the very end of the age."
(Matthew 28:16-20)

For the Bottom Line

Faith, Football, Star Power, and Even Greater Things

*This southern story from deep in the heart,
*Offers up wisdom for endings that can create a new start.

*In the biggest Alabama town where I-65, 59, 22 and 20 collide,
*God guides a "Magic City" so southern stars can reside.

*Gene Bartow started football with Coach Hilyer, then Brown,
    Callaway and McGhee,
*New beginnings saw winnings along with pitfalls hard to see.

*Bill Clark came just in the nick of time to turn it all around,
*Installing a victory mindset so that positive results could be found.

*In 2014 Coach Clark captured bowl eligibility for his first year
    as just a start,
*But suddenly heard rumors followed by a death blow to the heart.

*The Blazer program was shut down, after Coach Clark's first
    season,
*Young lives messed around with no apparent rhyme or reason.

*Players, coaches and support staff across the nation scattered,
*Young men in "The Pittsburgh of the South" found themselves
    beaten, bruised and battered.

*But Jesus resurrects more than you can even imagine in your
    mind,
*Including a city's university football team brought back with
    gifts of every kind.

*Coach Clark then commissioned a staff to become fishers of men,
*Reeling in great football players that sometimes mightily wres-
    tled with sin.

*Notre Dame Ex-Running Back Greg Bryant was the new UAB
    poster child destined for fame,
*But tragically got murdered on Mother's Day in Miami and never
    played a game.

*For more than 2 years the Blazers grind out on being prepared,
*The first team of its kind to in 2 years be FBS competition
    worthy declared.

*Anticipation began to mount in the "Iron City" to extremes,
*While the rest of the world laughed picking UAB last out of 130
    FBS teams.

*Game days came with extraordinary success, as UAB played for
    the kids and carried the load;
*The resurging Blazers were unbeatable at Legion field but sus-
    pect on the road.

*2017 saw a perfect record at home, 8-4 overall and history
   having been made;
*Then a Bahama Bowl for Christmas but a mystery on how
   poorly UAB played.

*2018 came and they said the Blazers "snuck up" on them all in 17,
*So…the Blazers stuck up 11 wins for that season doing things
   no one had ever seen.

*By God's grace from shutdown to Conference-USA Champions
   UAB was led,
*Capping 2018's championship Christmas with a bowl win instead.
*Many wins would come in 2019 even after 34 seniors departed
   who were known for talent and to be big hearted,
*Verifying once again that He who began a good work in us all
   will always complete what He started.

*Christ raised this team from the dead and His word is true,
*He did it for Birmingham and He will do it for you.

*Since we know God's word is true for us throughout eternities,
*How good it is to know that Christ himself said, "…they will do
   even greater things than these."

*It could be now or it may be later at UAB or another venue,
*But one way or another the resurrection power of Christ will
   always continue.

*Not sure about this story? Then Google "UAB Football
  Resurrection" and plainly see,
*How Jesus' resurrection power in all our stories will change
  your destiny.

*And if you wonder why before every line in this poem aster-
  isks * appear,
*Those asterisks represent the stars of this extraordinary story
  from whom you may never hear.

CPSIA information can be obtained
at www.ICGtesting.com
Printed in the USA
LVHW052010220720
661200LV00005B/260

9 781630 501044